HELLO, ADVENTURE FRIENDS!

WE ARE A SMALL COMPANY WITH BIG DREAMS, AND WE'VE
CREATED THIS BOOK WITH LOTS OF LOVE JUST FOR YOU.

WE WHOLEHEARTEDLY HOPE YOU ENJOY EVERY PAGE, EVERY
WORD, EVERY ILLUSTRATION, IMMERSING YOURSELVES IN
ADVENTURES THAT MAKE YOU DREAM AND SMILE. IF, UPON
CLOSING THIS BOOK, YOU FEEL THAT SPARK OF JOY, COULD YOU
SHARE YOUR EXPERIENCE BY LEAVING US A REVIEW? IT REALLY
HELPS A SMALL COMPANY LIKE OURS.

THANK YOU FOR SHARING YOUR MAGIC WITH US!

Hello adventurers! Are you ready for an exciting journey through time? Put on yo explorer hats because today we're going to uncover the secrets of Ancient Egypt!

Many, many years ago, even before the existence of cell phones and television, there wa: magical place called Egypt. Did you know that Egypt is a country located on a contine called Africa? Well, Ancient Egypt was very special because it was right next to a huge a famous river called the Nile. This river was like a superhighway connecting all the people and cities.

In Ancient Egypt, people built incredible things. Have you heard of the pyramids? They were like mountains made by humans!
The most famous are the pyramids of Giza, and the largest one is called the Great Pyramid. Can you imagine building something so big without cranes or modern machinery?
The Egyptians were super ingenious!

...t that's not all; the Egyptians also worshiped many gods and goddesses, each with their ...scinating powers and stories. For instance, there was Ra, the sun god, who lit up the sky ...ch day with his solar boat. Or Isis, a very powerful and wise goddess. And let's not forget ...nubis, with the head of a jackal, who looked after people on their journey to the afterlife.

The pharaohs were like the kings and queens of Egypt. One very famous pharaoh was Tutankhamun, who was only nine years old when he began to rule! Imagine being a king or queen at that age. The pharaohs were so important that when they died, they were mummified and placed in tombs filled with treasures and paintings.

Speaking of paintings, the Egyptians wrote with pictures called hieroglyphs. It was like a secret code with images of animals, people, and things. It was their way of telling stories and keeping records!

Ancient Egypt is full of mysteries and wonders. Who knows what else you might discover on your adventures? Stay curious and learn a lot!

INDEX

DAILY LIFE

CHAPTER 1

magine walking under the warm Egyptian sun. To keep cool, the Egyptians wore lightweight clothing made of linen, a fabric derived from plants of the Nile. Men wore short skirts, and women wore long, straight dresses.

And let's not forget the colorful necklaces, bracelets, and earrings!

Jewelry was not just for looking good; it also displayed a person's wealth and social status.

FESTIVALS AND CELEBRATIONS

The Egyptians loved to celebrate. They had festivals to give thanks to the gods, celebrate the harvests, and honor their pharaohs. At these festivals, there was music, dancing, and games.

Musicians played flutes, lyres, and drums, while dancers moved to the rhythm of the music, often in vibrant and colorful costumes.

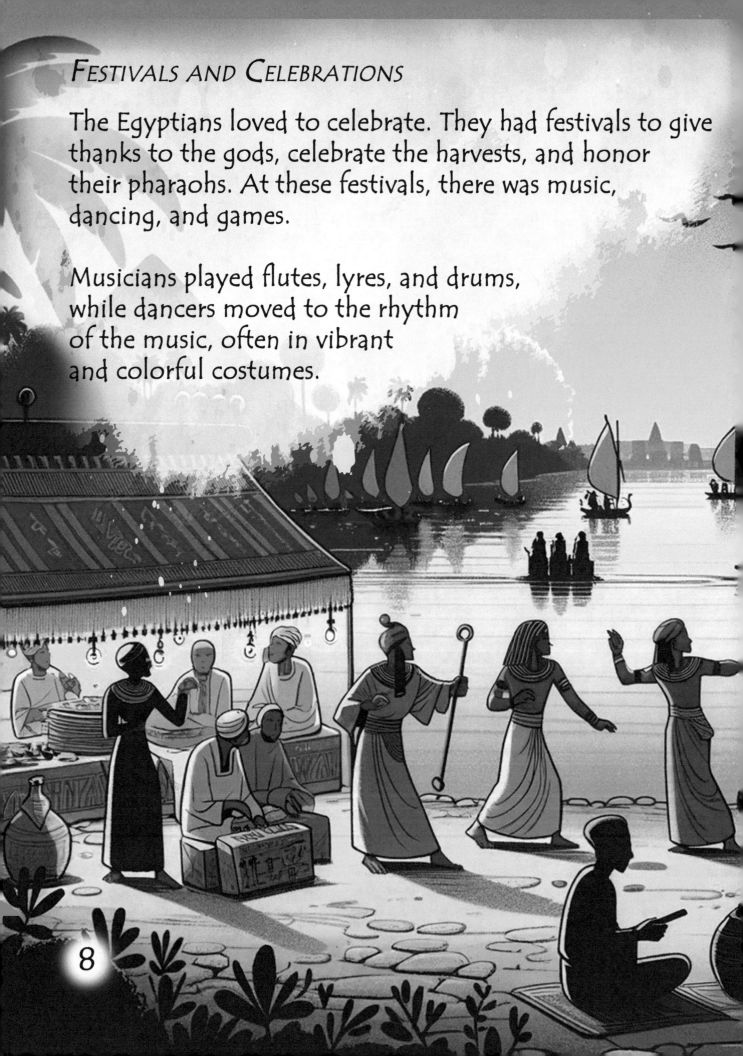

Wondering what the Egyptians ate? Their diet was quite simple but nutritious. Bread and beer were staples, supplemented by onions, garlic, lentils, and cucumbers.

Fish from the Nile was very common, although meat was more of a luxury for special occasions.

And for dessert, fruits like dates and figs!

SPORTS AND GAMES

The Egyptians knew how to have fun too!

Children and adults played board games like Senet, which was somewhat like today's chess. They also engaged in sports such as wrestling, archery, and swimming.

Even sports competitions were held during the festivals.

11

A WATERWAY

The Nile was not only crucial for agriculture, but it also served as a major highway for the ancient Egyptians. They used boats to travel and transport goods along the river. Imagine seeing ships loaded with stones for building pyramids, grains, fruits, and even huge monuments.

The Nile was Egypt's supermarket and highway!

Along the Nile, people lived, worked and played. Fishermen with nets and rods sought fish, while farmers tended to their green fields by the river's edge.

Children played and swam in the waters, always being careful not to disturb the hippos and crocodiles that also called the Nile home.

A Life-Giving River

But why is the Nile so important? Well, in ancient Egypt, the land was very dry and it was hard to grow food. But every year, the Nile would overflow and leave behind black, fertile mud, perfect for planting wheat and barley. Thanks to this, the Egyptians had enough food for the whole year.

The Nile was like a huge food pantry!

The Nile River is like a gigantic snake slithering through Egypt. With its length of 6,650 kilometers, it's the longest river in the world. Imagine this:

It's so long that you could place almost 60,000 soccer fields end to end along the river!

15

ARTISANS AND MERCHANTS

In the cities, we would find artisans and merchants.

Artisans were skilled workers such as carpenters, jewelers, and potters who created beautiful works of art.

Merchants sold and bought products, and sometimes traveled far to exchange goods with other cultures.

16

THE HEART OF EGYPT: THE FARMERS

Most people in ancient Egypt were farmers. They worked in the fields, growing wheat and barley, and raising animals like sheep and cows.

The farmers depended on the Nile River to irrigate their crops and make the land fertile.

THE SCRIBES: THE WISE OF THE KINGDOM

In ancient Egypt, being able to read and write was a great privilege.
This is where the scribes come in, highly educated people who wrote letters, kept records, and accounted for the kingdom's wealth.

The scribes used hieroglyphs, a type of writing with drawings and symbols.

The Soldiers: Protectors of the Kingdom

The Egyptian soldiers protected the country from invaders and helped the pharaoh conquer new lands.

They were brave and strong, and used weapons like spears, shields, and bows.

AT THE TOP: THE PHARAOH

Imagine a grand throne in a golden palace. There sits the pharaoh, the king or queen of Egypt, considered a god on Earth.

The pharaoh had absolute power and was responsible for making laws, leading wars, and maintaining peace.

He was the most important figure in all of Egypt!

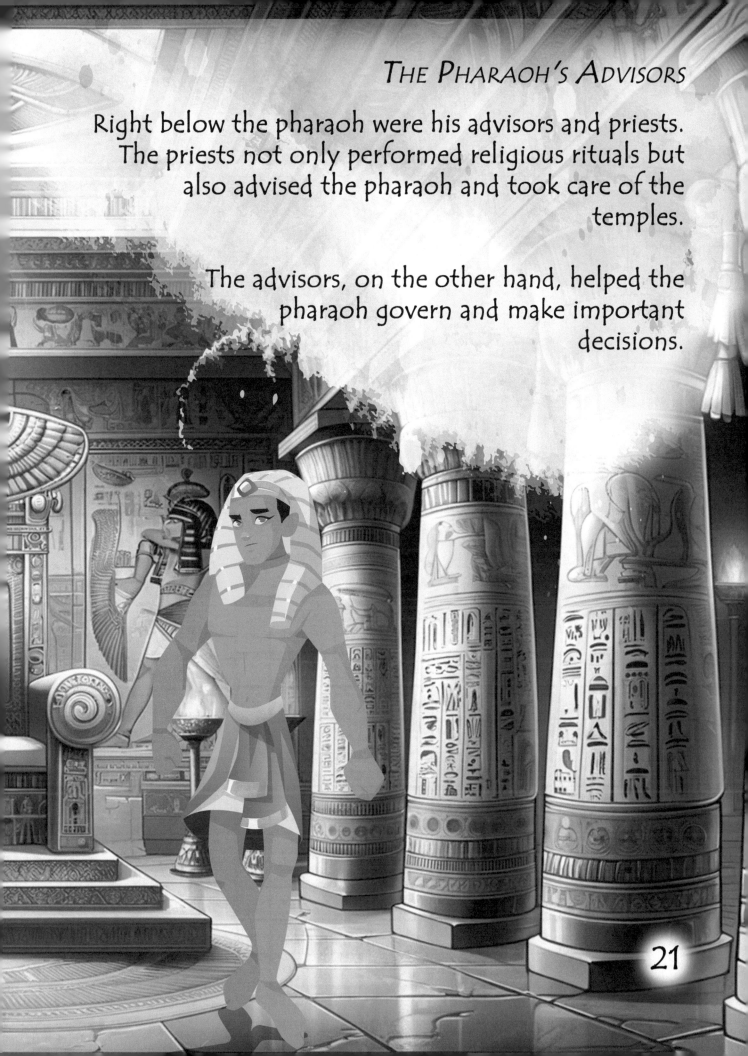

THE PHARAOH'S ADVISORS

Right below the pharaoh were his advisors and priests. The priests not only performed religious rituals but also advised the pharaoh and took care of the temples.

The advisors, on the other hand, helped the pharaoh govern and make important decisions.

21

FIND THE 7 DIFFERENCES BETWEEN THE TWO IMAGES:

FIND THE FOLLOWING 6 WORDS IN THE NEXT WORD SEARCH:

F	E	K	D	A	T	E	S	E	S	X	M
P	S	S	J	F	K	G	D	J	B	G	F
H	C	L	W	N	U	J	N	V	W	D	Q
A	R	D	O	E	H	I	S	L	C	Y	Z
R	I	G	F	B	L	S	M	T	N	G	F
A	B	J	K	E	O	R	M	J	J	G	B
O	E	C	R	O	C	O	D	I	L	E	O
H	Z	B	N	W	W	G	G	G	R	R	X
J	T	P	R	R	O	Z	B	J	X	W	N
S	E	N	E	T	X	Y	B	W	U	N	I
S	S	Q	X	G	L	L	Y	K	L	K	H
M	D	A	P	I	G	T	P	I	K	Q	M

- NILE
- SENET
- CROCODILE
- SCRIBE
- PHARAOH
- DATES

PHARAOHS

CHAPTER 2

WHO WERE THESE "SUPER-KINGS"?

The pharaohs were much more than mere kings; they were seen as gods on Earth. They ruled Egypt with absolute power and were responsible for everything from making laws to leading wars.

The Egyptians believed that the pharaohs were descendants of the god Ra, the sun god, and that's why they respected and worshiped them.

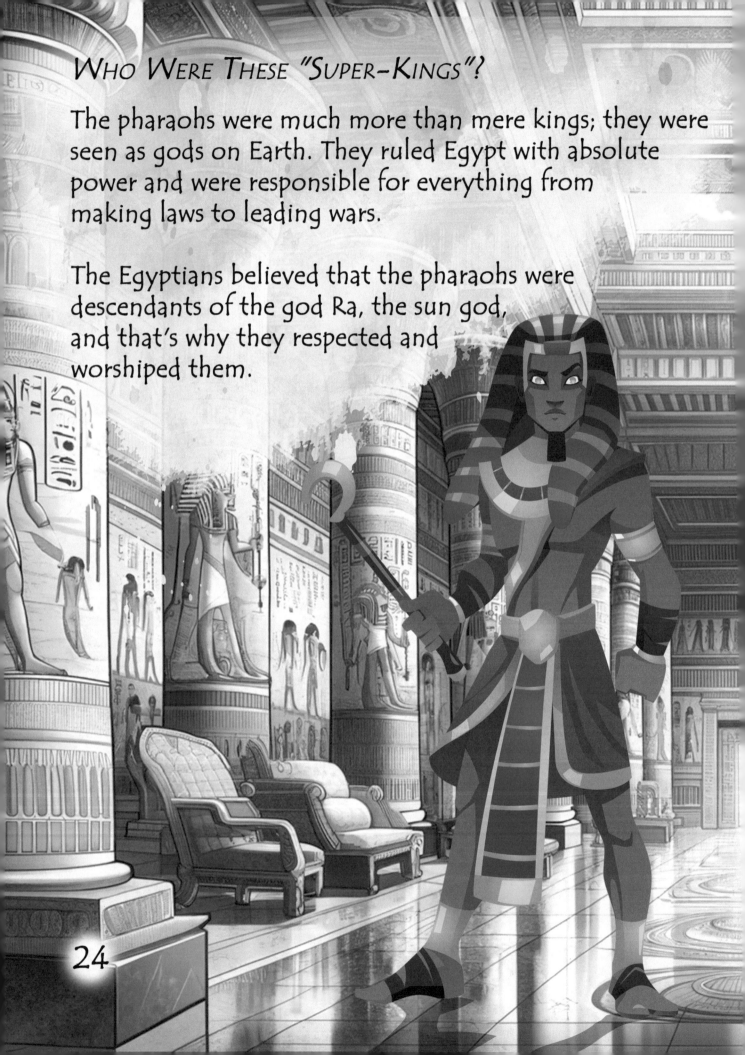

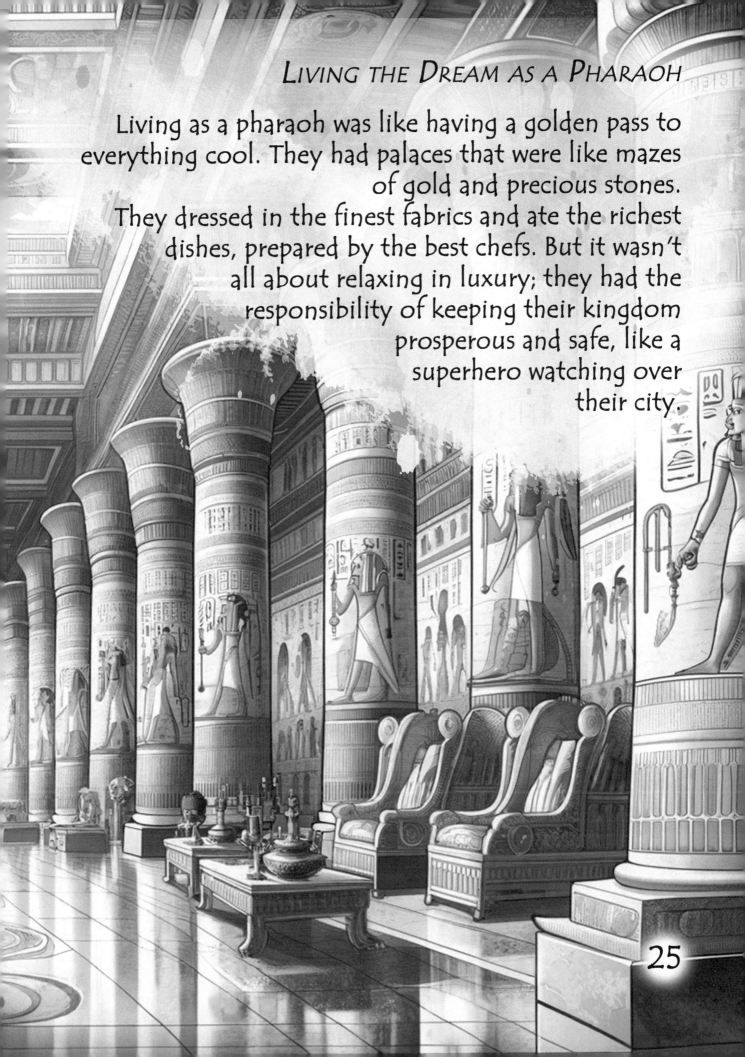

Living as a pharaoh was like having a golden pass to everything cool. They had palaces that were like mazes of gold and precious stones. They dressed in the finest fabrics and ate the richest dishes, prepared by the best chefs. But it wasn't all about relaxing in luxury; they had the responsibility of keeping their kingdom prosperous and safe, like a superhero watching over their city.

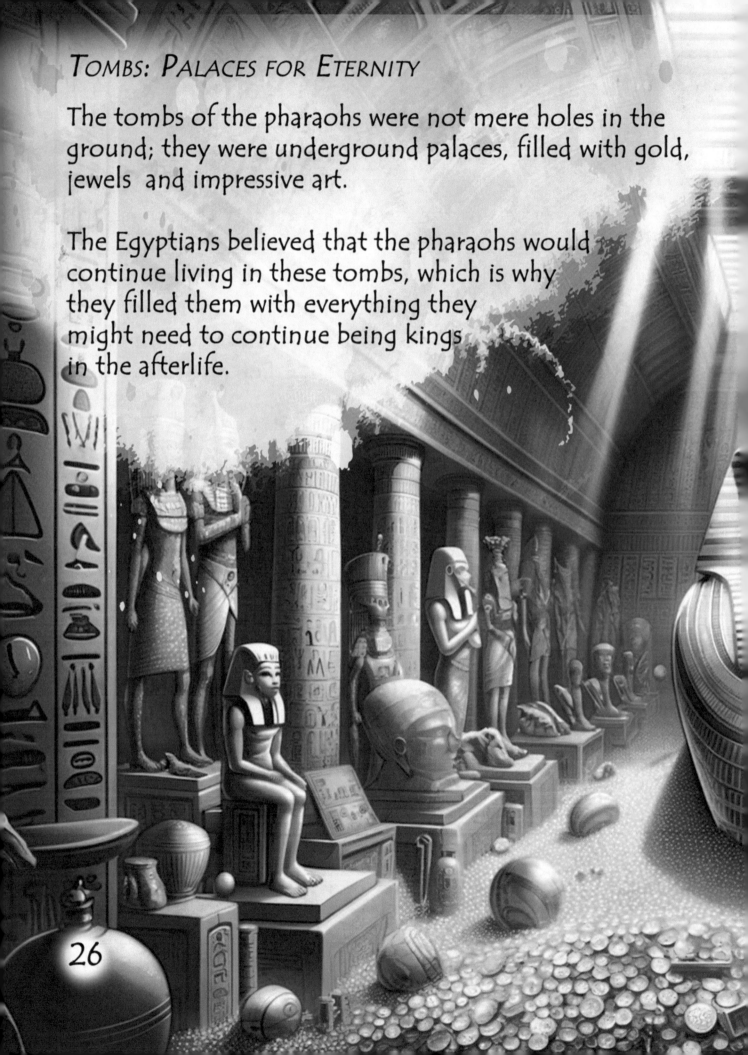

TOMBS: PALACES FOR ETERNITY

The tombs of the pharaohs were not mere holes in the ground; they were underground palaces, filled with gold, jewels and impressive art.

The Egyptians believed that the pharaohs would continue living in these tombs, which is why they filled them with everything they might need to continue being kings in the afterlife.

26

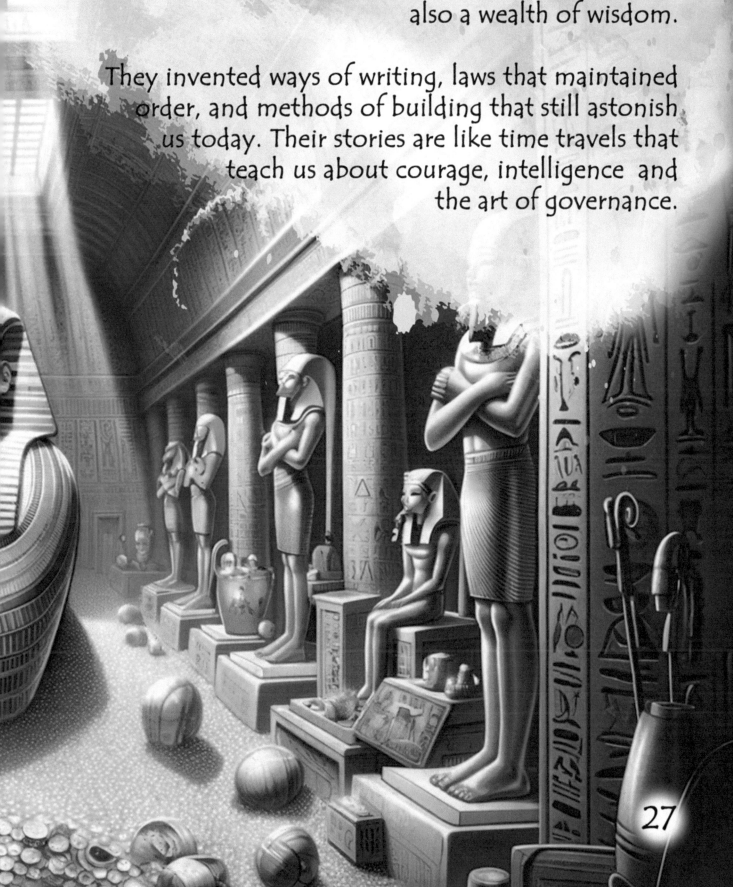

The pharaohs left us not only pyramids and treasures but also a wealth of wisdom.

They invented ways of writing, laws that maintained order, and methods of building that still astonish us today. Their stories are like time travels that teach us about courage, intelligence and the art of governance.

27

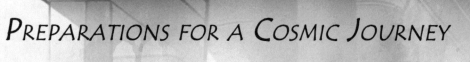

PREPARATIONS FOR A COSMIC JOURNEY

For the Egyptians, death was just the beginning of a new grand life. When a pharaoh died, impressive ceremonies and rituals were prepared, as if they were sending a king into space.

It was their ticket to the stars of the afterlife!

THE END OF THE PHARAOHS

The era of the pharaohs came to an end when Egypt was conquered by the Roman Empire.

But Egypt's story didn't end there. Throughout the centuries, Egypt has been part of many empires and has seen the birth of many cultures and traditions.

MUMMIFICATION: THE POWER TO LAST FOREVER

Mummification was a process to keep bodies in perfect condition.

Specialists carefully removed organs that could decay and dried the body. Then, they wrapped it in bandages as if it were a special gift for the gods.

This was their way of ensuring that the pharaoh was ready and perfect for his new life.

Who Was Cleopatra?

Over 2,000 years ago, in the land of pharaohs and mythological gods, lived Cleopatra, the last queen of Ptolemaic Egypt. She was not just a queen; she was an intelligent leader, a skillful politician and a great scholar.

She spoke several languages and was knowledgeable about mathematics, astronomy, and medicine!

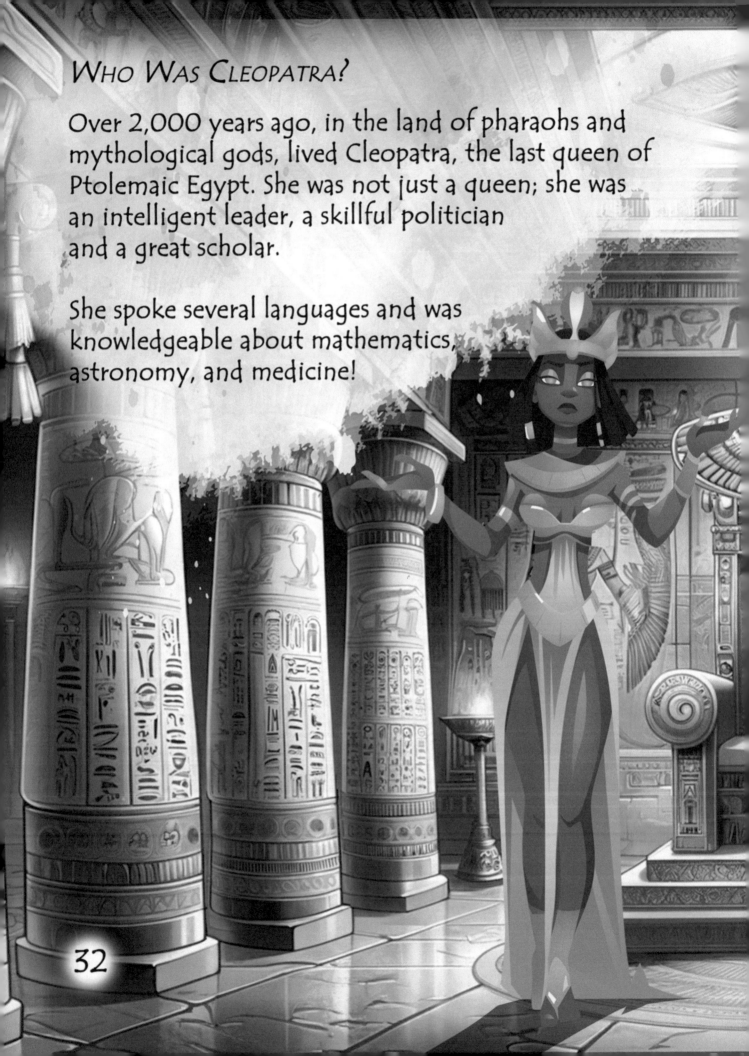

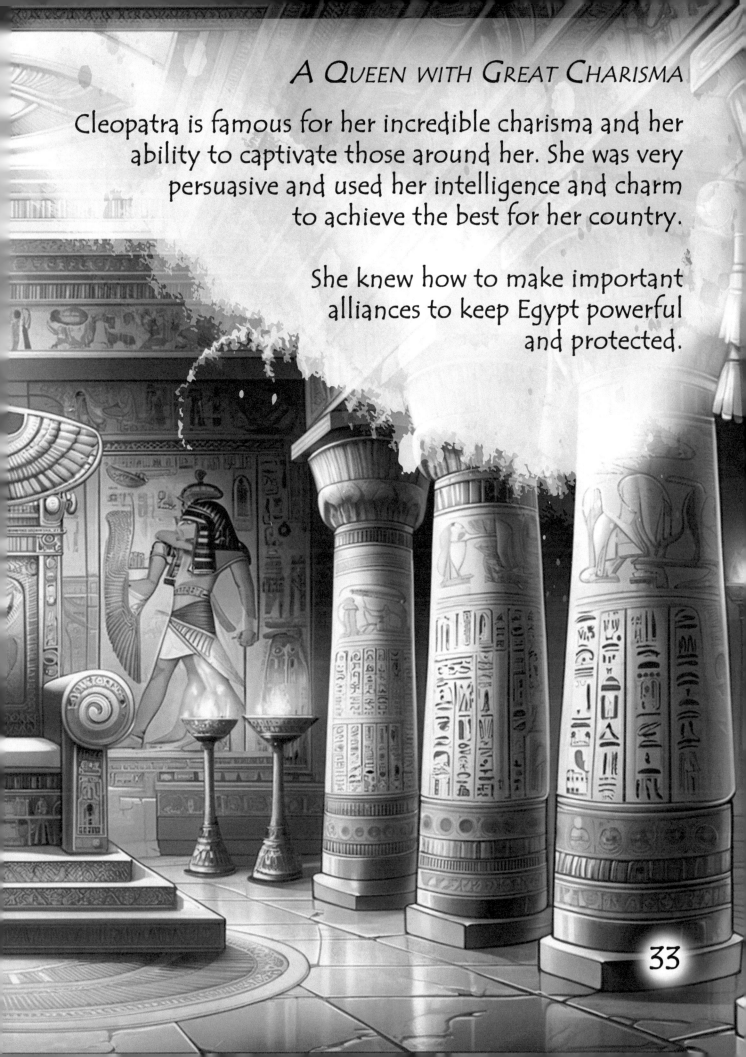

A Queen with Great Charisma

Cleopatra is famous for her incredible charisma and her ability to captivate those around her. She was very persuasive and used her intelligence and charm to achieve the best for her country.

She knew how to make important alliances to keep Egypt powerful and protected.

33

ALLIANCES AND LOVES

The most intriguing aspect of Cleopatra was her alliances with powerful Roman leaders. First, she formed a relationship with Julius Caesar, an important general and leader of Rome. Later, she allied herself with Mark Antony, another highly influential Roman leader.

These alliances were part of her strategy to protect Egypt from being conquered by Rome.

The story of Cleopatra is both glamorous and tragic. After a series of political events and battles, Cleopatra and Mark Antony faced the forces of Rome in a great battle.

Unfortunately, they lost, marking the end of Cleopatra's reign and the beginning of Roman control over Egypt.

Cleopatra was not only the last queen of Ptolemaic Egypt but also one of the most remembered women in ancient history.

Her life has inspired numerous stories, plays and movies.

Through her intelligence, leadership, and charm, she left a mark that has transcended time.

WHO WAS CHEOPS?

Over 4,500 years ago, in ancient Egypt, a powerful pharaoh named Cheops ruled. He was the second pharaoh of the Fourth Dynasty, a time when Egypt was very wealthy and powerful.

Cheops is especially famous for building the Great Pyramid of Giza, a feat that still astonishes us today.

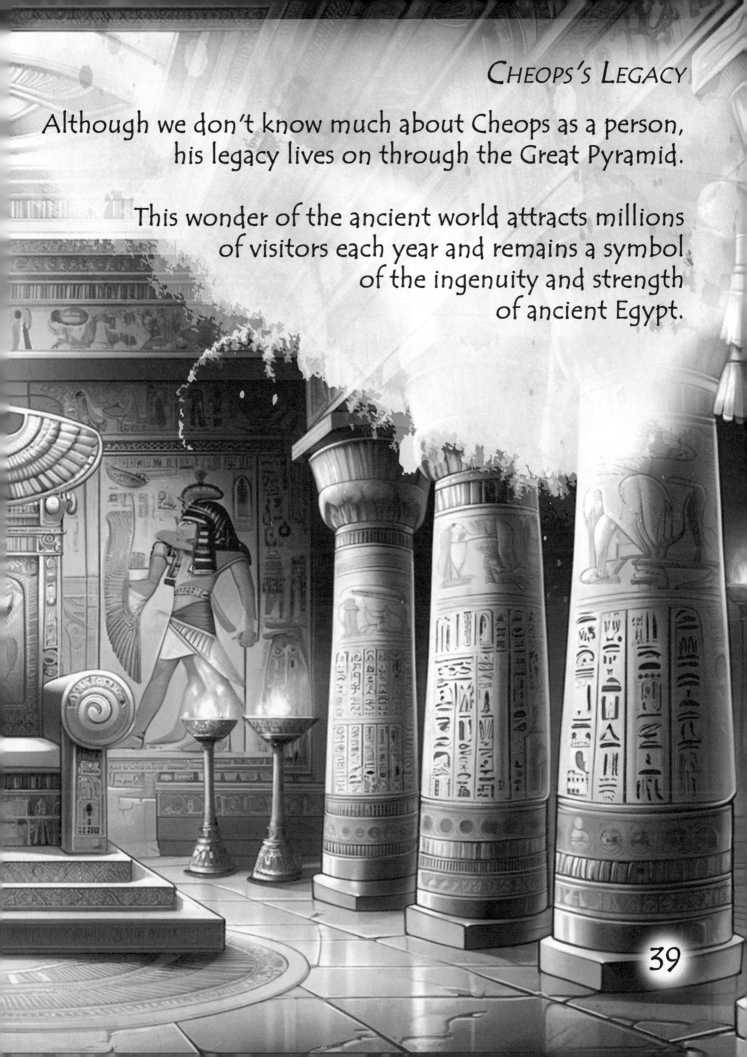

Although we don't know much about Cheops as a person, his legacy lives on through the Great Pyramid.

This wonder of the ancient world attracts millions of visitors each year and remains a symbol of the ingenuity and strength of ancient Egypt.

How Was the Pyramid Built?

The ancient Egyptians didn't have cranes or modern machinery, so building the Great Pyramid was a colossal challenge.

It's believed they used ramps, sledges and a lot of human strength. Thousands of workers collaborated on this great project, which took about 20 years to complete.

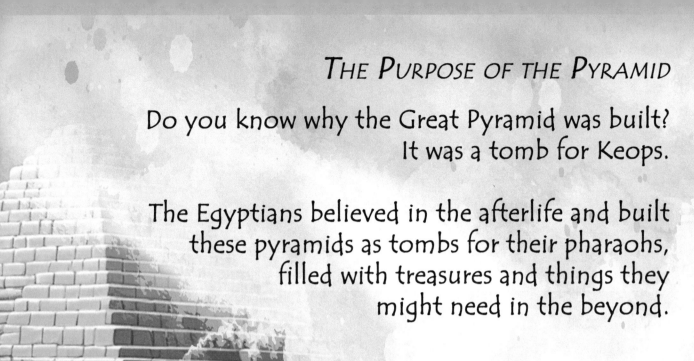

THE PURPOSE OF THE PYRAMID

Do you know why the Great Pyramid was built?
It was a tomb for Keops.

The Egyptians believed in the afterlife and built
these pyramids as tombs for their pharaohs,
filled with treasures and things they
might need in the beyond.

41

THE GREAT PYRAMID

The Great Pyramid is gigantic: it originally measured about 146 meters in height.

That's almost as tall as a 50-story building!

It was the tallest man-made structure for thousands of years.

The most impressive part about its construction is that it was built with stone blocks that weighed as much as elephants!

Who Was Ramses II?

Over 3,000 years ago, in the land of pyramids and pharaohs, lived a king named Ramses II.

But he was no ordinary king! Ramses II was one of the most powerful and famous pharaohs of all Egypt.

He ruled for 66 years! Imagine, it's like being in school for more than 60 years!

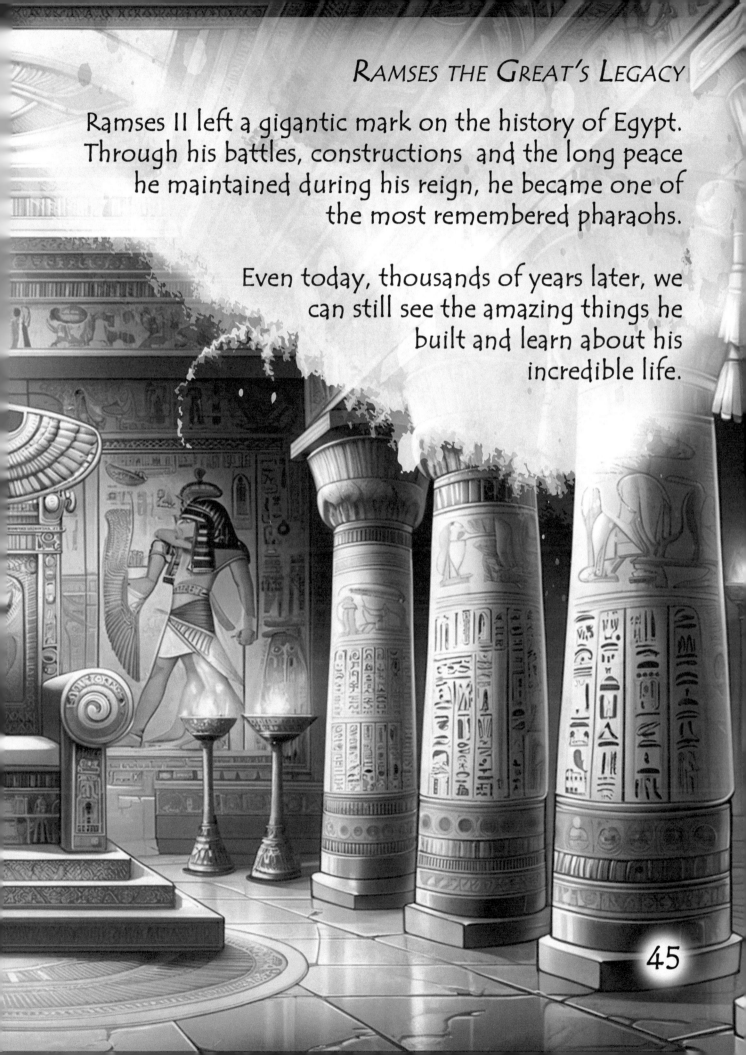

Ramses II left a gigantic mark on the history of Egypt. Through his battles, constructions and the long peace he maintained during his reign, he became one of the most remembered pharaohs.

Even today, thousands of years later, we can still see the amazing things he built and learn about his incredible life.

But Ramses wasn't just a warrior; he was also an incredible builder.

He loved having gigantic statues of himself and marvelous temples constructed. One of his most amazing projects was the temple of Abu Simbel.

Imagine two giant temples carved directly into the rock with statues of Ramses that are over 20 meters high!

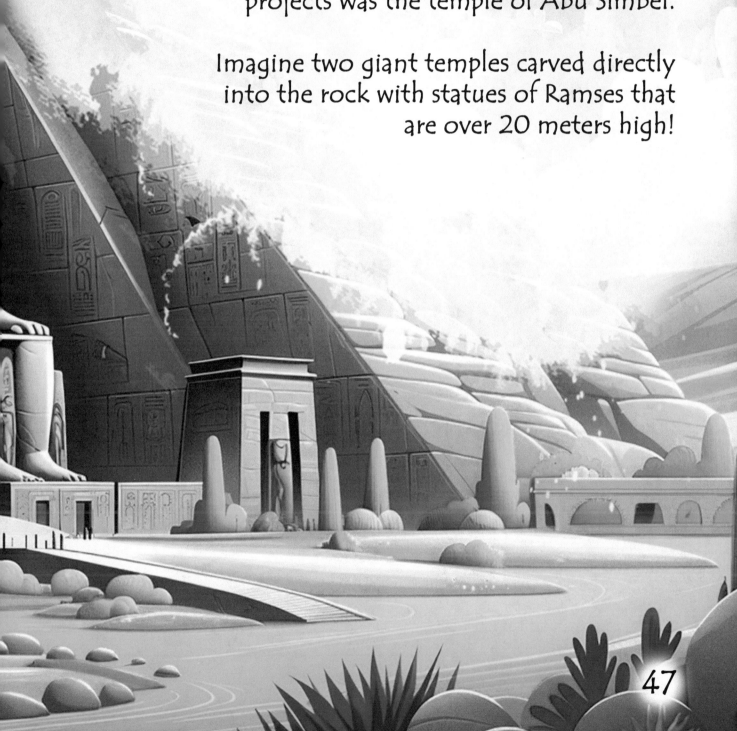

An Adventurous Pharaoh

Ramses II loved adventures. He was a great leader in battles, fighting to protect Egypt from other countries.

One of his most famous battles was the Battle of Kadesh. Though it was a tough fight, Ramses used his cunning and bravery to face his enemies.

He was like a superhero of ancient Egypt!

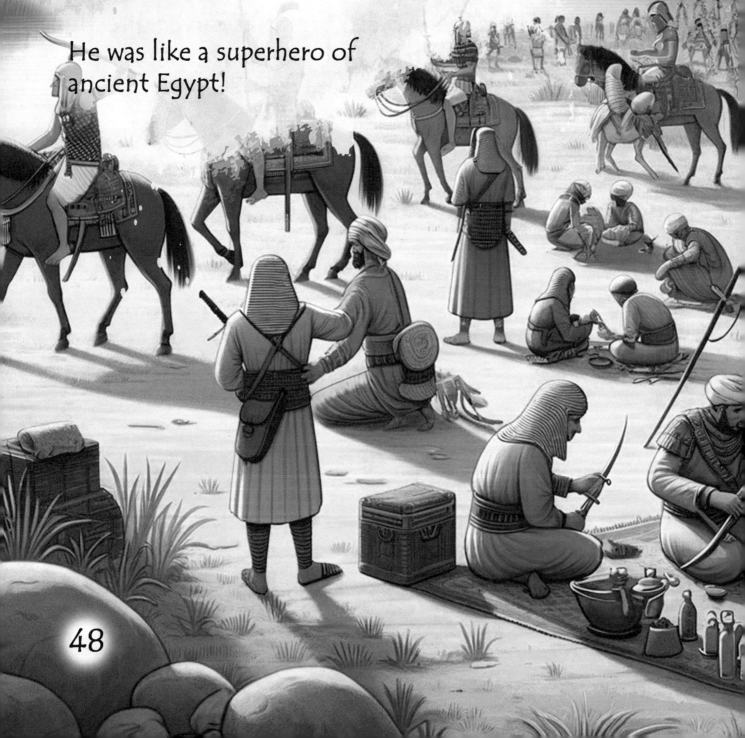

Ramses also loved his family dearly. He married his great love, Nefertari and together they had many children.

He even built a special temple at Abu Simbel for Nefertari, showing how much he adored her.

49

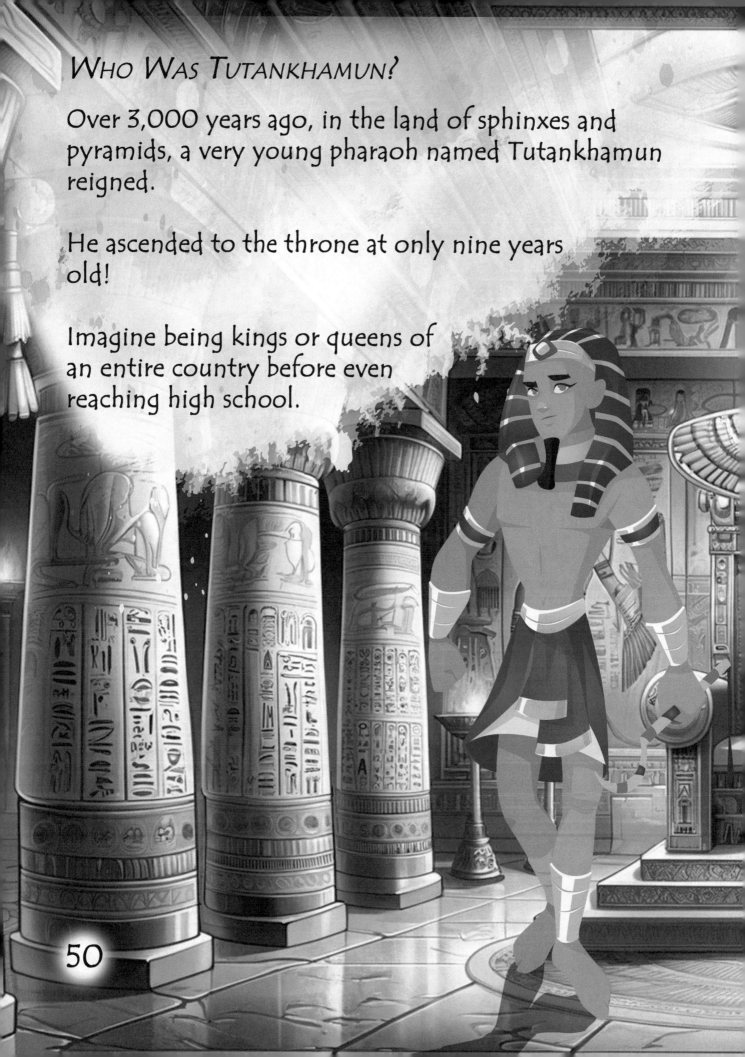

WHO WAS TUTANKHAMUN?

Over 3,000 years ago, in the land of sphinxes and pyramids, a very young pharaoh named Tutankhamun reigned.

He ascended to the throne at only nine years old!

Imagine being kings or queens of an entire country before even reaching high school.

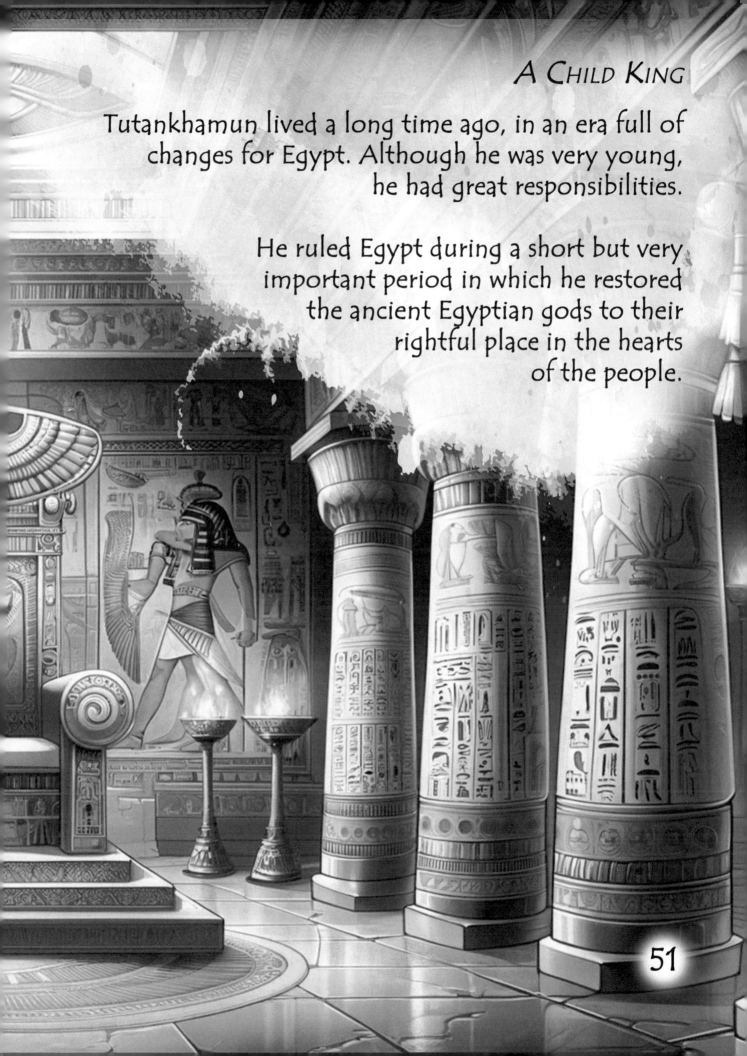

A CHILD KING

Tutankhamun lived a long time ago, in an era full of changes for Egypt. Although he was very young, he had great responsibilities.

He ruled Egypt during a short but very important period in which he restored the ancient Egyptian gods to their rightful place in the hearts of the people.

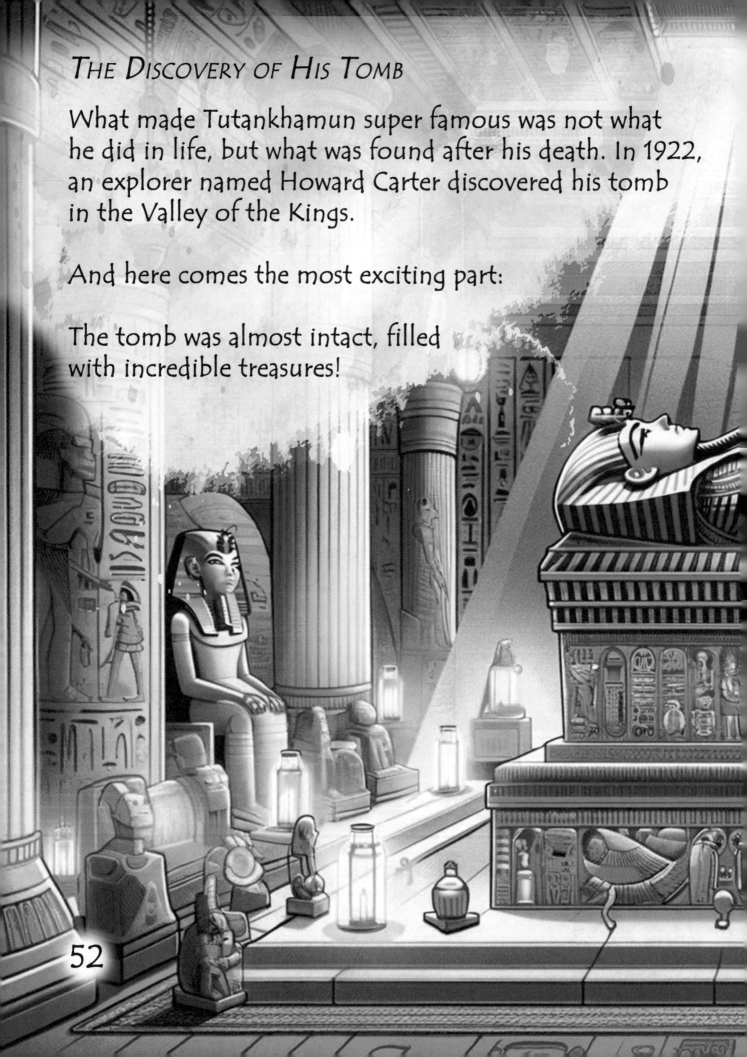

THE DISCOVERY OF HIS TOMB

What made Tutankhamun super famous was not what he did in life, but what was found after his death. In 1922, an explorer named Howard Carter discovered his tomb in the Valley of the Kings.

And here comes the most exciting part:

The tomb was almost intact, filled with incredible treasures!

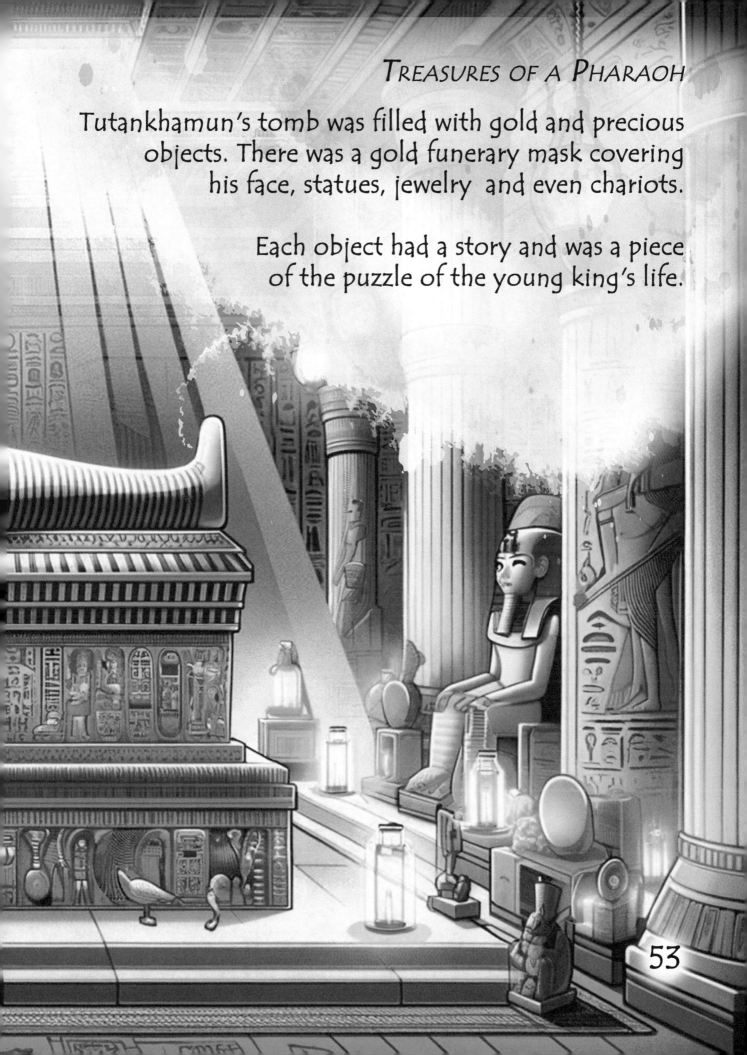

Tutankhamun's tomb was filled with gold and precious objects. There was a gold funerary mask covering his face, statues, jewelry and even chariots.

Each object had a story and was a piece of the puzzle of the young king's life.

THE MYSTERY OF HIS DEATH

The young pharaoh died when he was about 19 years old, and for a long time, his death was a great mystery.

Some thought it was an accident, while others believed in stranger theories.

The truth is that even today, scientists are trying to uncover what really happened.

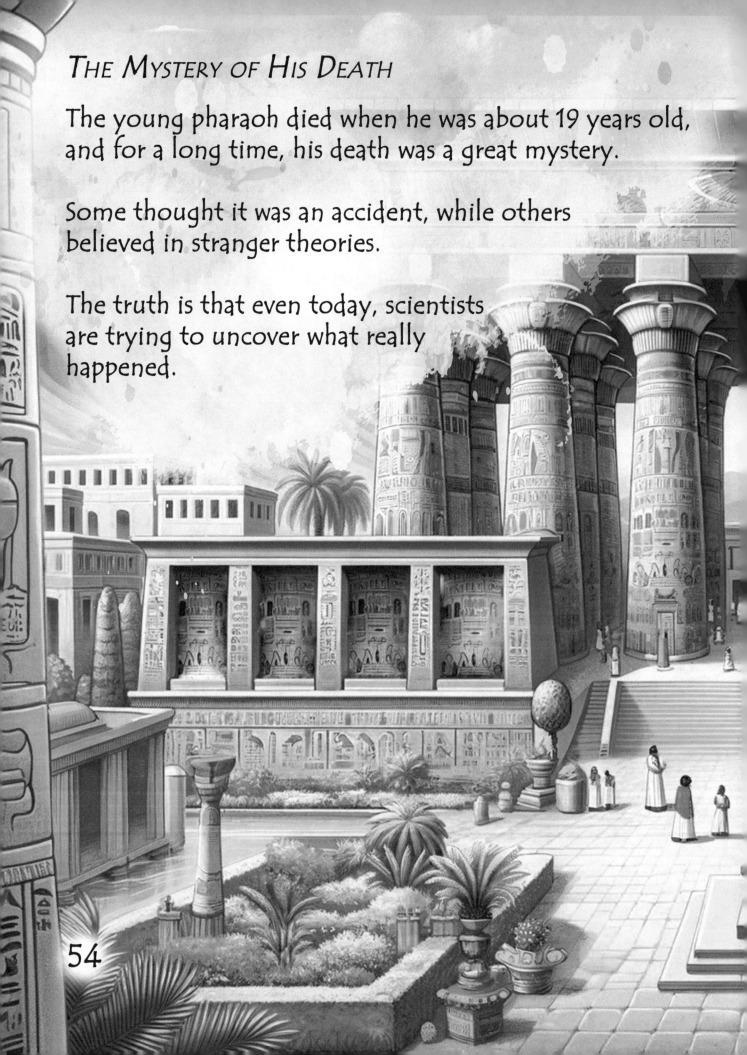

Although Tutankhamun was not the most powerful pharaoh nor did he reign the longest, his tomb gave us a window to the past and taught us a lot about how the ancient Egyptians lived.

Today, Tutankhamun is one of the most famous pharaohs, and his name is synonymous with mystery and treasure.

55

GAMES

FIND THE PATH INSIDE THE MAZE TO GATHER THE PHARAOHS.

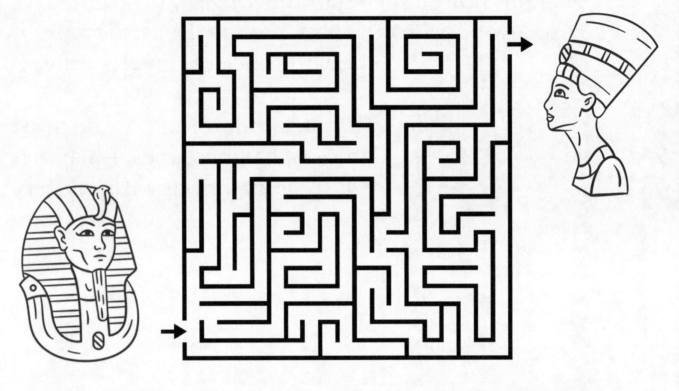

FILL IN THE FOLLOWING CROSSWORD WITH THE 6 MISSING WORDS:

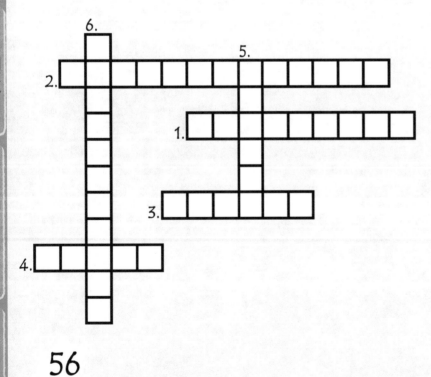

1. THE MOST IMPORTANT WOMAN IN ANCIENT EGYPT.

2. PROCESS TO PRESERVE BODIES AFTER DEATH.

3. PHARAOH WHO BUILT THE GREAT WONDER OF ABU SIMBEL.

4. EMPIRE WITH WHICH CLEOPATRA ACHIEVED A GREAT ALLIANCE.

5. PHARAOH WHO CREATED THE PYRAMIDS OF GIZA.

6. PHARAOH WHO ASCENDED TO THE THRONE AS A CHILD.

56

GODS
CHAPTER 3

57

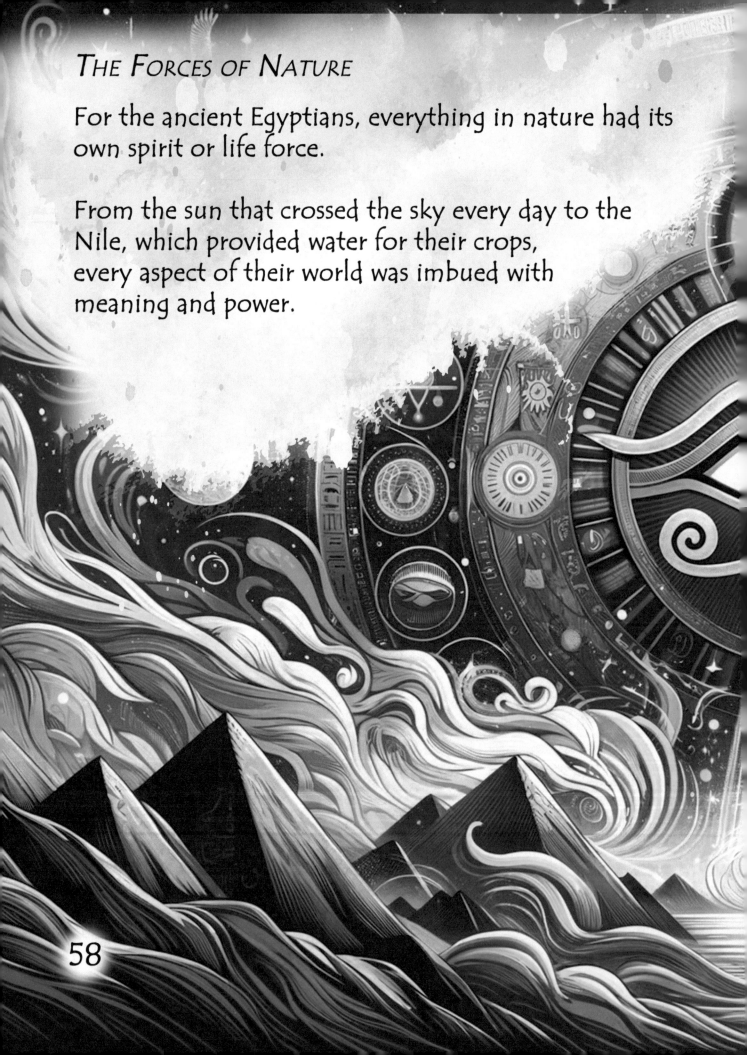

THE FORCES OF NATURE

For the ancient Egyptians, everything in nature had its own spirit or life force.

From the sun that crossed the sky every day to the Nile, which provided water for their crops, every aspect of their world was imbued with meaning and power.

A WORLD FULL OF MAGIC AND MYSTERY

Ancient Egypt was a place where the magical and the everyday intertwined.

People from this ancient civilization believed that the world was filled with powerful forces and beings that influenced their daily lives, from birth to after death.

PROTECTORS AND GUIDES

At the heart of their beliefs were the powerful beings that ruled over all aspects of the universe.

These beings not only had control over natural elements, such as the sun, the moon and the river, but they also influenced people's daily lives, protecting them, guiding them and sometimes even punishing them.

Through fascinating stories, the ancient Egyptians explained how the world worked. These stories spoke of battles between opposing forces, magical journeys, and acts of heroism and betrayal.

They were a way to teach important values and explain the mysteries of life and death.

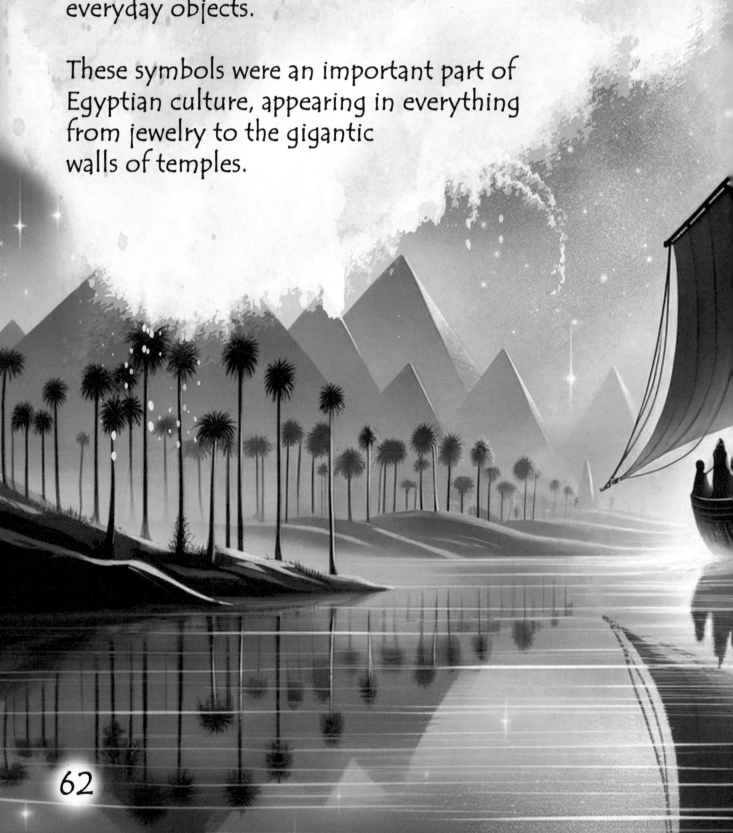

A WORLD OF SYMBOLS

Each of these powerful beings was associated with specific symbols that represented them in art, architecture and everyday objects.

These symbols were an important part of Egyptian culture, appearing in everything from jewelry to the gigantic walls of temples.

LIFE AFTER DEATH

One of the most important beliefs in ancient Egypt was the afterlife.

The Egyptians believed that after dying, they would embark on a journey to the other world, where powerful beings would judge their actions and decide their fate.

WHO WAS AMUN?

Amun, the King of the Gods in ancient Egypt, was often depicted as a man with a ram's head or wearing a crown with two long plumes.

Revered as the god of the wind and mystery, Amun filled the world with his invisible yet omnipresent essence, serving as a symbol of the mystical and the incomprehensible.

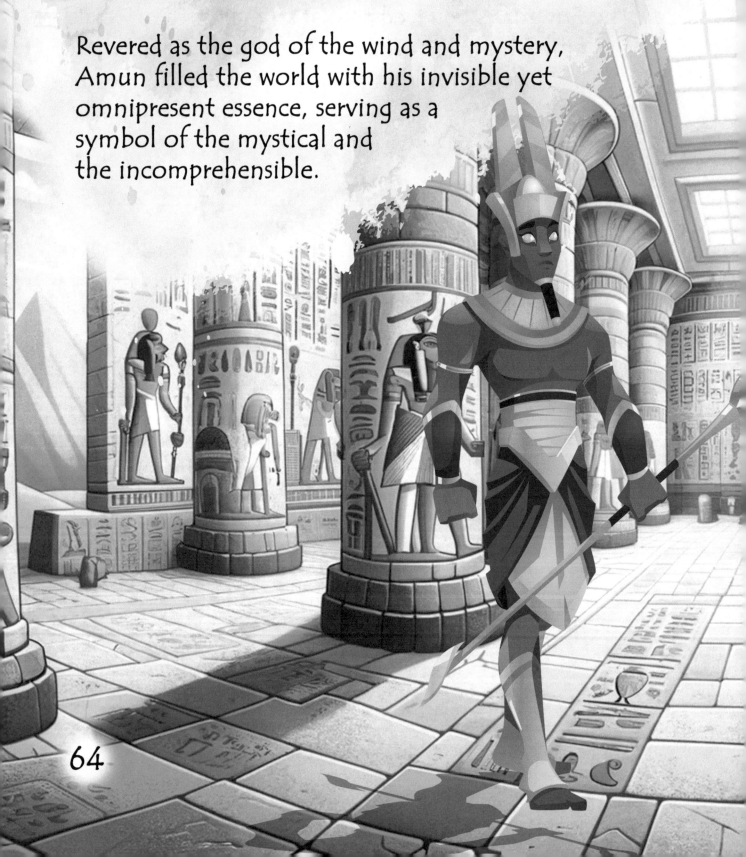

The worship of Amun reached its zenith in Thebes, especially at the Karnak temple complex, securing his position as the divine protector of Egypt and its pharaohs.

His fusion with Ra, the sun god, created Amun-Ra, a supreme deity worshipped as the creator of the universe.

Amun was not only the guardian of kings but also a god close to the common people, who prayed to him for protection and guidance in everyday life.

WHO WAS ANUBIS?

Anubis is one of the most intriguing gods of ancient Egypt. With the head of a jackal and the body of a human, he was the protector of graves and the guide of souls in the afterlife.

Anubis had a very important job: to ensure that the journey to the other world was safe for the deceased.

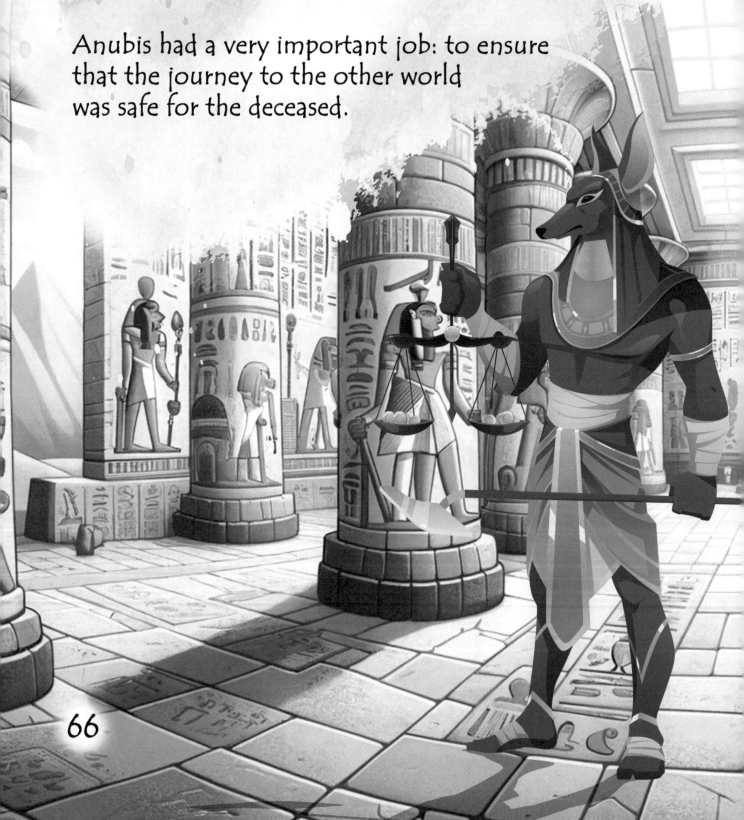

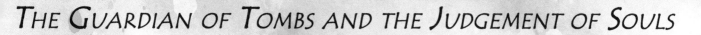

THE GUARDIAN OF TOMBS AND THE JUDGEMENT OF SOULS

As a guardian of tombs, Anubis protected the deceased from thieves and oversaw the mummification process, preparing them for the afterlife.

During the judgement of souls, he weighed the heart of the deceased against a feather, a process that emphasized the importance of justice and truth.

Although his figure might seem intimidating, Anubis was deeply revered, trusted to guide and protect the deceased in the afterlife.

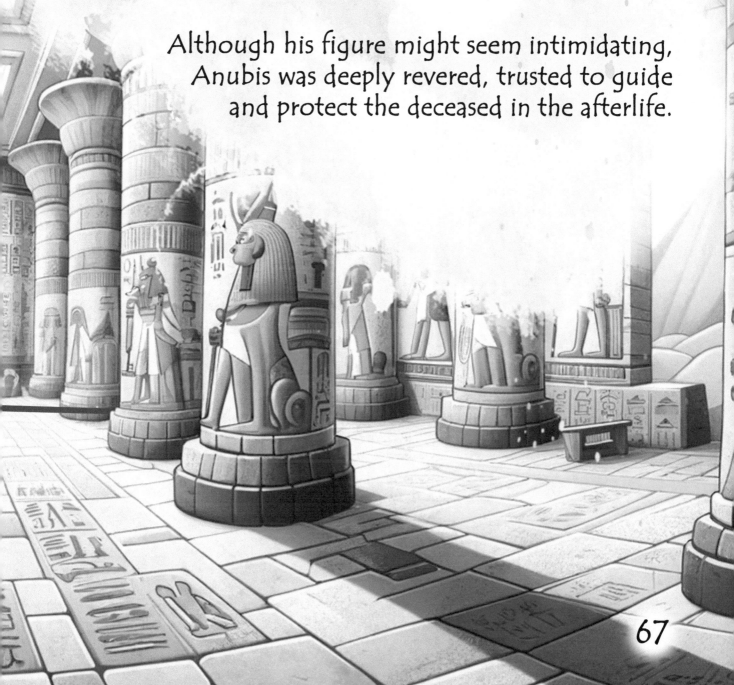

WHO WAS HATHOR?

Hathor was the goddess of love, beauty, music, dance, and joy in ancient Egypt.

She was depicted as a beautiful woman with cow horns and a solar disk between them, symbolizing her connection with the sky and the sunlight.

Recognized for her kindness, Hathor was the protector of women and children, ensuring they receive love and care. As the goddess of music and dance, she inspired joy and celebration among the Egyptians, filling their festivities with songs and laughter in her honor.

Hathor reminded everyone to enjoy life and take care of each other, with temples dedicated to her as places of happiness and unity.

Hathor also played a crucial role in the afterlife, welcoming souls with music and joy, and offering them eternal comfort.

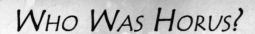

WHO WAS HORUS?

Horus, a key deity in Egyptian mythology, was depicted as a man with the head of a falcon or as a falcon itself.

He symbolized the sky, the protection of the realm and was considered a source of power and light, with a vision that spanned the entire world.

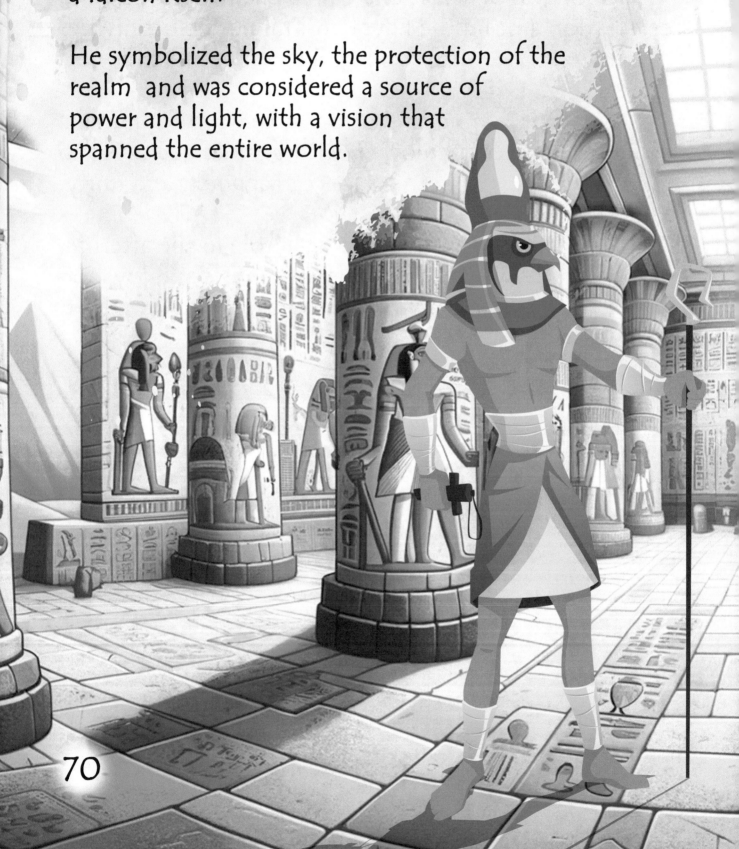

Horus is celebrated for his heroic battle against the god of chaos to avenge his father and secure his place as the legitimate ruler of Egypt.

This legend underscores his bravery and his crucial role as a defender of order. Horus also influenced the pharaohs, who were seen as his earthly incarnation, bearing his title as a symbol of legitimacy and justice.

Additionally, Horus was revered for his protective and healing powers, symbolized by his two eyes, representing the sun and the moon. His worship brought people together, filling his temples with offerings and keeping his story alive through generations.

Who was Isis?

Isis was a prominent Egyptian goddess, revered for her magical powers, her role as protector of motherhood and fertility.

The ancient Egyptians considered her capable of offering special protection to mothers and children thanks to her supernatural abilities.

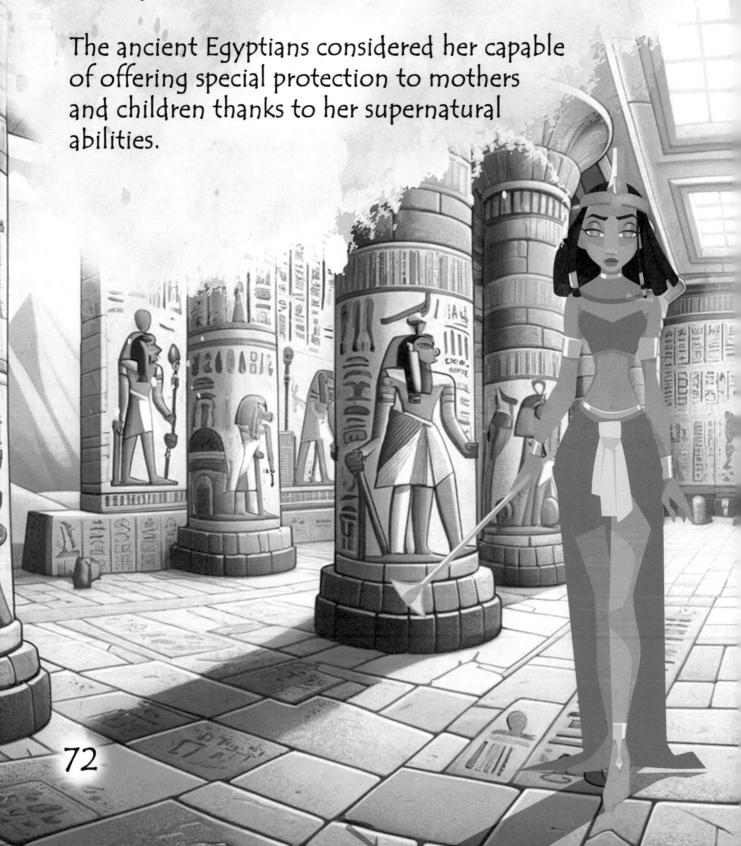

Isis was not only famous for her magic, used to safeguard her family and heal diseases but also for being a deeply loved deity.

Admired for her intelligence, bravery, and compassion, she was seen as a mother to all of Egypt. Although the stories of ancient Egypt have passed thousands of years ago, the figure of Isis remains a symbol of love, protection, and magic.

Her story teaches us about the power of care and the importance of family.

WHO WAS OSIRIS?

Osiris stood out among the Egyptian gods as the lord of the afterlife and deity of agriculture and vegetation.

Not only did he teach humans to cultivate the land, but he also provided them with laws for harmonious coexistence.

His fascinating legend encompasses themes of life, betrayal, death and a miraculous rebirth.

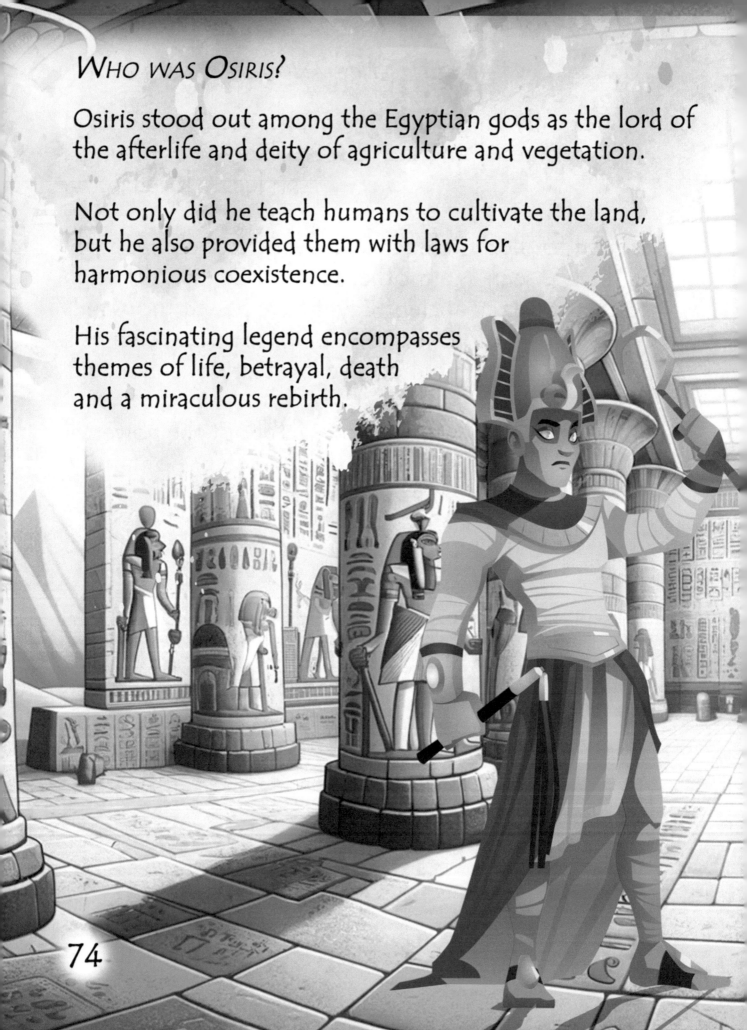

Osiris, revered as a just and benevolent king, suffered betrayal and death, but was magically revived to rule the afterlife.

As judge of the souls, he decided who deserved eternal paradise, emphasizing the importance of kindness and purity of heart.

Symbolizing the natural cycle of life, death, and rebirth, Osiris played a crucial role in agriculture and was deeply worshipped for providing fertility to the land and justice to the people, being honored in temples and rituals throughout Egypt

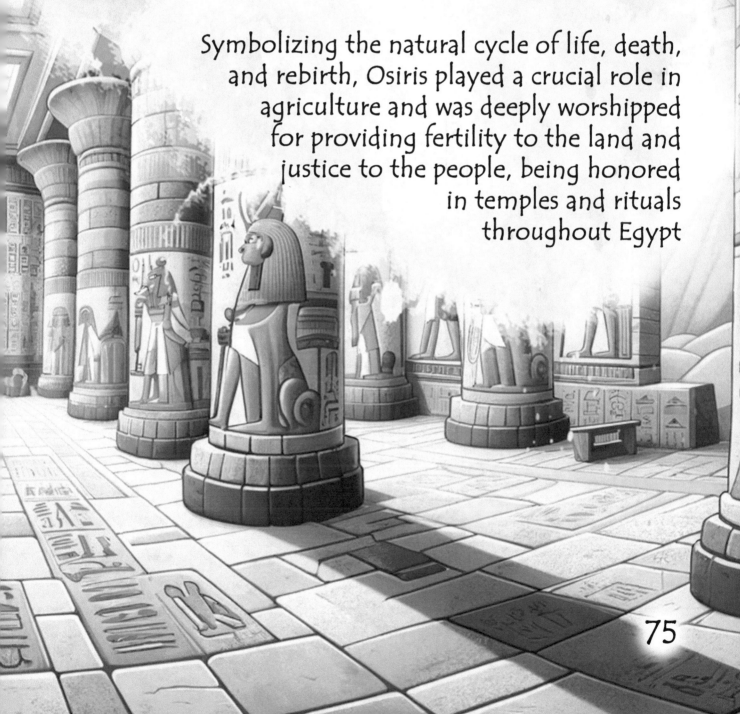

Who was Ra?

In ancient Egypt, Ra was the sun god, the most powerful and radiant of all. The Egyptians believed that Ra traveled across the sky during the day in his solar barge, bringing light and warmth to the world.

As night fell, Ra continued his journey through the underworld, battling the forces of chaos to rise again the next day.

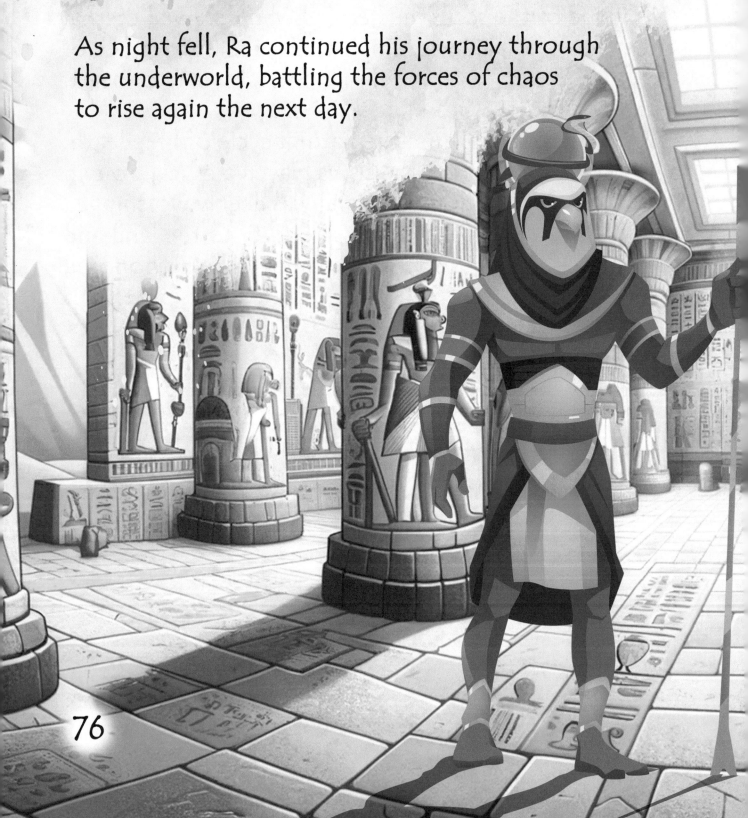

The sun, the source of all life, was intrinsically linked to Ra, whose heat and light allowed the survival and prosperity of the crops.

Besides his daily journey, Ra was known for his Watchful Eye, which defended the world from disorder. His presence extended to art and culture, depicted as a man with the head of a falcon and venerated in magnificent temples.

Ra was not only a symbol of power but also a fundamental pillar of daily life and Egyptian spirituality.

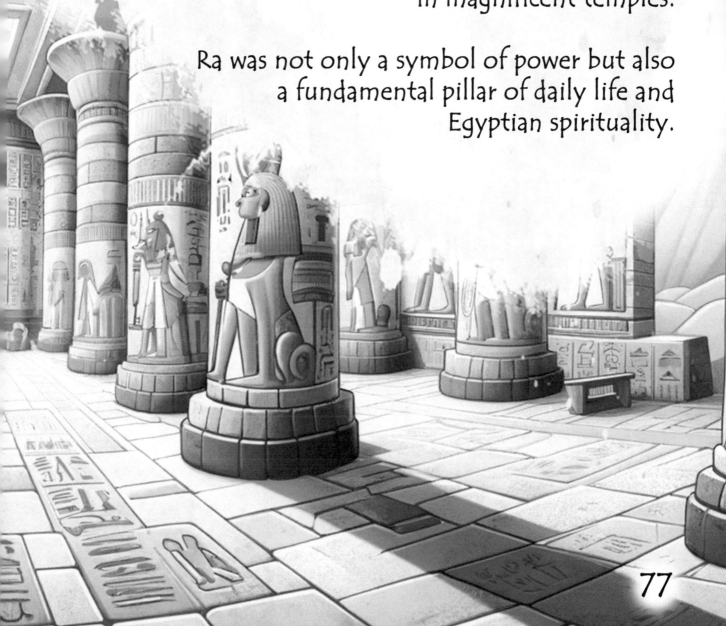

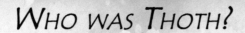

WHO WAS THOTH?

Thoth was the god of knowledge and writing in ancient Egypt, depicted as a man with the head of an ibis or baboon.

Considered the inventor of writing and guardian of knowledge, Thoth maintained the balance of the universe with his wisdom.

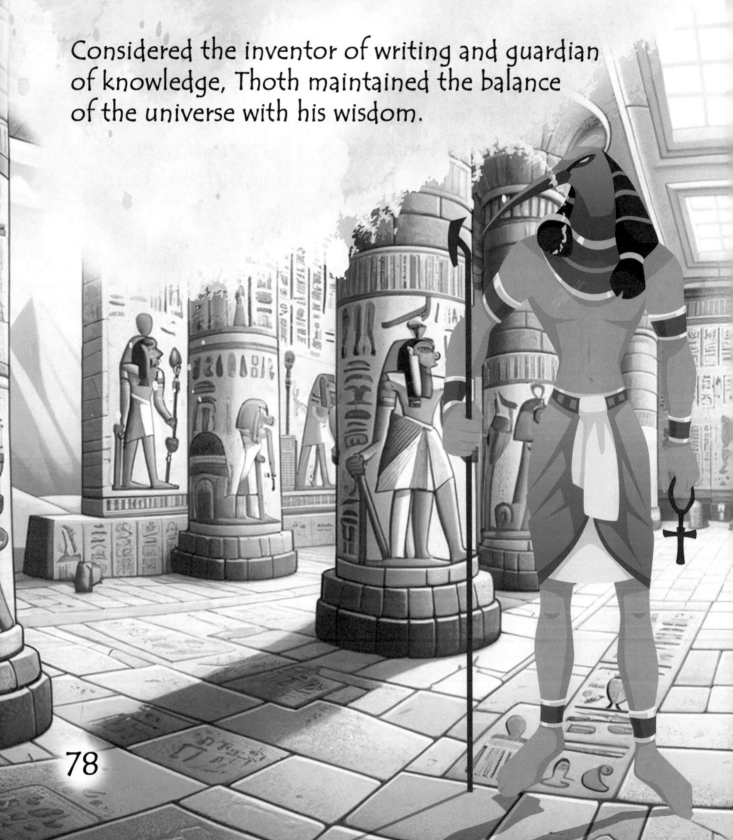

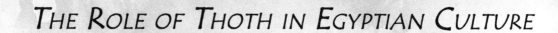

THE ROLE OF THOTH IN EGYPTIAN CULTURE

Thoth was the master of hieroglyphs, teaching humans to record their history and secrets.

Not only was he the advisor of the gods, but he also played a crucial role in the afterlife, recording the outcomes of the souls' judgment to ensure a fair process.

Admired for his intelligence, Thoth was the patron of scribes and a symbol of wisdom.

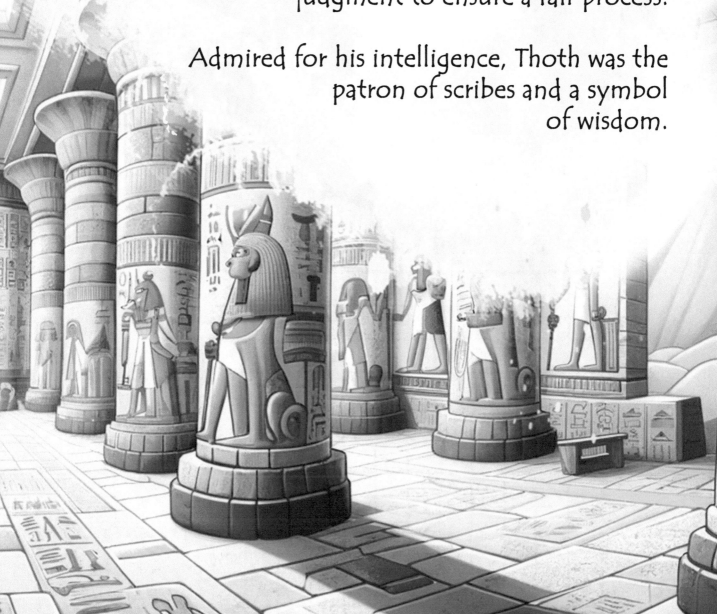

GAMES

Match the 8 Gods From the First Column to the Second:

· Anubis	Sun ·
· Amun	Underworld ·
· Hathor	Sky ·
· Horus	Wisdom ·
· Isis	Mummification ·
· Osiris	Love ·
· Ra	Wind ·
· Thoth	Maternity ·

Find in the Following Word Search the 8 Words:

W	C	W	F	B	M	J	R	K	M	H	W
P	V	E	Z	G	K	A	I	P	A	O	X
J	Y	R	O	S	I	R	I	S	N	R	W
M	E	H	Q	E	Y	H	O	M	U	U	L
C	W	A	I	H	I	J	Q	O	B	S	T
F	A	P	S	A	L	J	T	W	I	V	H
X	M	K	I	T	Z	L	I	W	S	A	O
G	K	R	S	H	U	D	R	Y	M	H	T
Q	R	H	G	O	K	C	X	U	N	K	H
R	A	X	N	R	N	N	N	Q	U	W	P
Z	I	E	Z	G	P	M	A	R	J	Z	Z
X	M	D	R	X	N	Y	D	T	G	O	L

· Anubis

· Amun

· Hathor

· Horus

· Isis

· Osiris

· Ra

· Thoth

80

ART AND STRUCTURES

CHAPTER 4

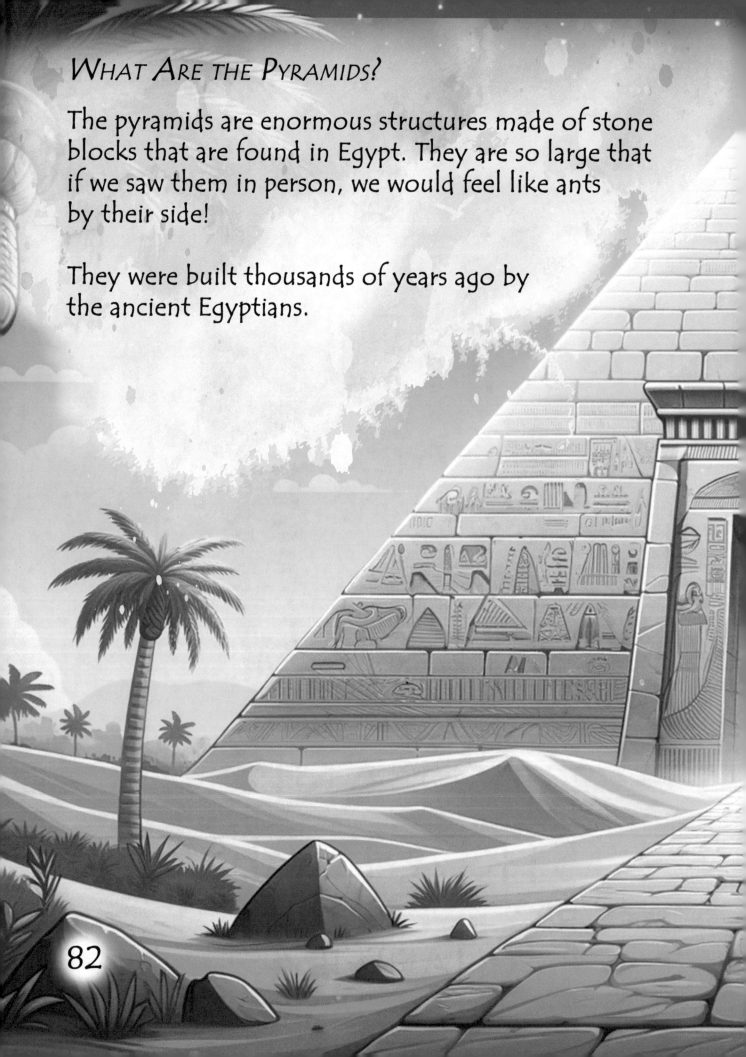

WHAT ARE THE PYRAMIDS?

The pyramids are enormous structures made of stone blocks that are found in Egypt. They are so large that if we saw them in person, we would feel like ants by their side!

They were built thousands of years ago by the ancient Egyptians.

82

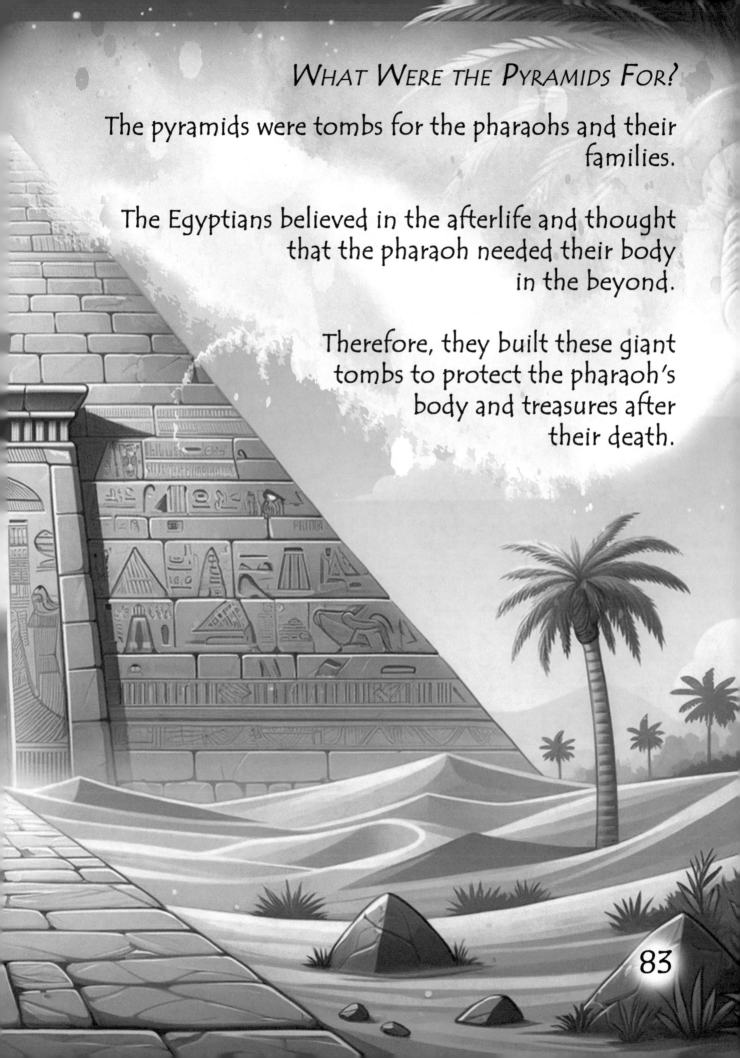

WHAT WERE THE PYRAMIDS FOR?

The pyramids were tombs for the pharaohs and their families.

The Egyptians believed in the afterlife and thought that the pharaoh needed their body in the beyond.

Therefore, they built these giant tombs to protect the pharaoh's body and treasures after their death.

How Were the Pyramids Built?

Building a pyramid was a gigantic project. The Egyptians did not have modern machinery, so how did they do it?

They used stone blocks that they cut and carved in quarries. Then, they transported them to the construction site, probably using sleds and rollers. Workers used ramps to place each block in its place.

84

Although we know a lot about how the pyramids were built, there are still many mysteries to solve.

How did the Egyptians achieve such precision and perfection?

Each pyramid is a puzzle that we are still trying to fully understand.

THE GREAT PYRAMID OF GIZA: Built by Pharaoh Khufu, it is the largest of all the pyramids and one of the Seven Wonders of the Ancient World. It originally stood at 146 meters high, nearly as tall as a 50-story building.

THE PYRAMID OF KHAFRE: It is the second pyramid at Giza and appears taller than Khufu's because it is built on higher ground. It retains some of its original limestone casing at the top.

THE PYRAMID OF MENKAURE: It is the smallest of the three pyramids of Giza and is famous for its complex design and the statues found within.

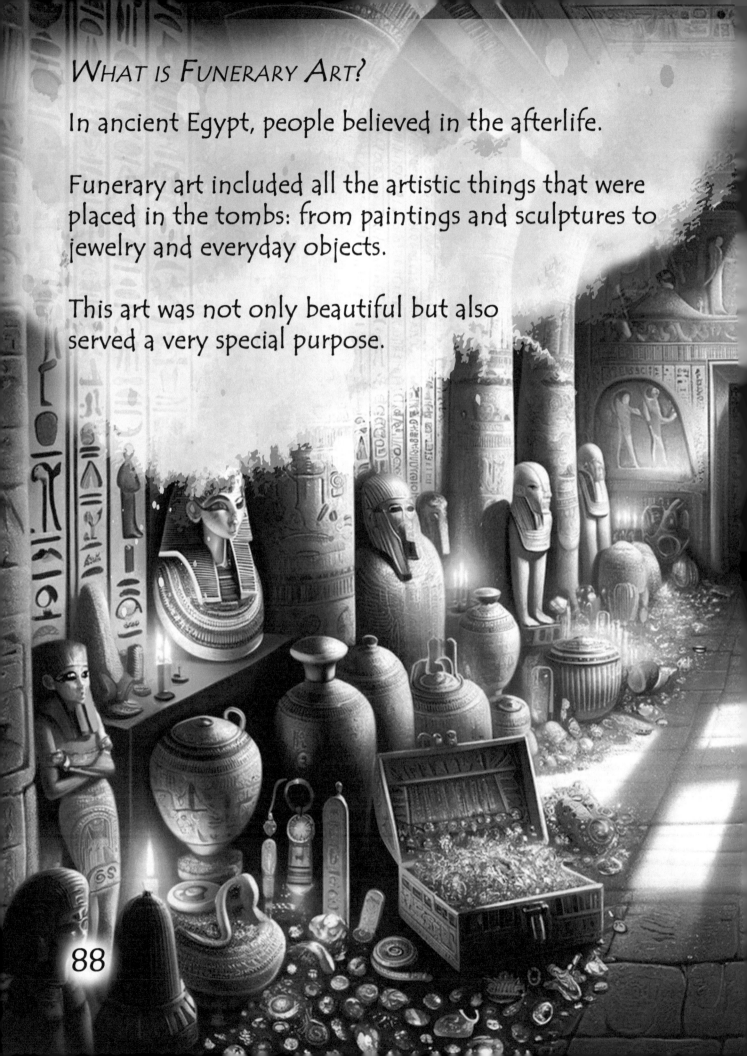

WHAT IS FUNERARY ART?

In ancient Egypt, people believed in the afterlife.

Funerary art included all the artistic things that were placed in the tombs: from paintings and sculptures to jewelry and everyday objects.

This art was not only beautiful but also served a very special purpose.

88

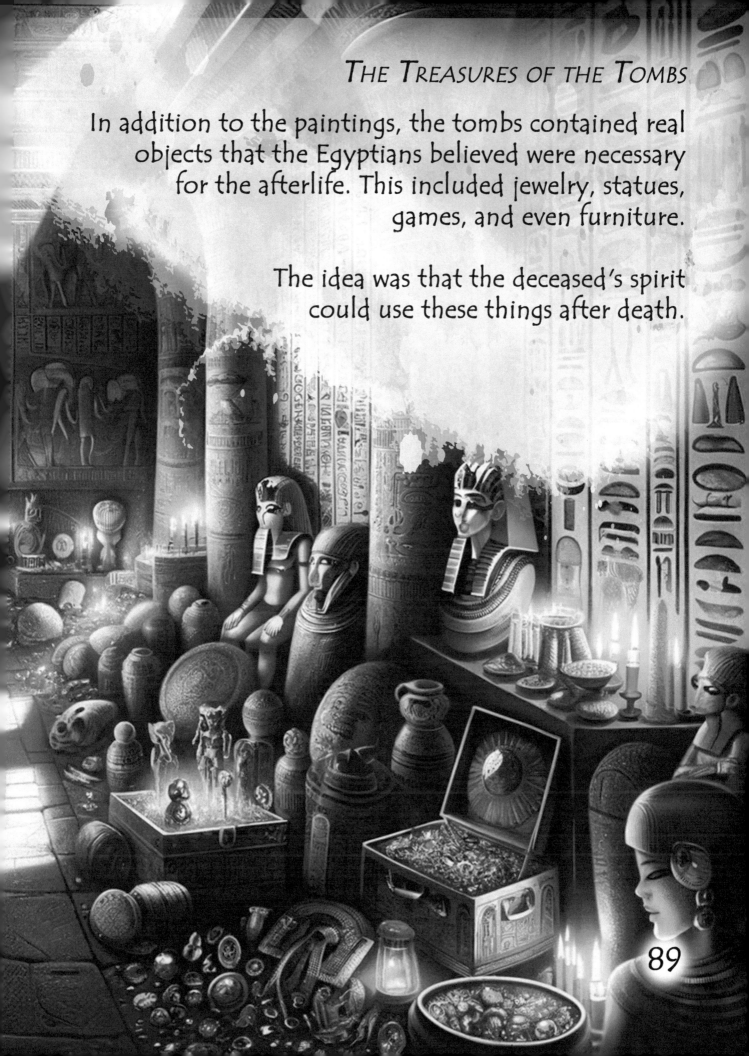

THE TREASURES OF THE TOMBS

In addition to the paintings, the tombs contained real objects that the Egyptians believed were necessary for the afterlife. This included jewelry, statues, games, and even furniture.

The idea was that the deceased's spirit could use these things after death.

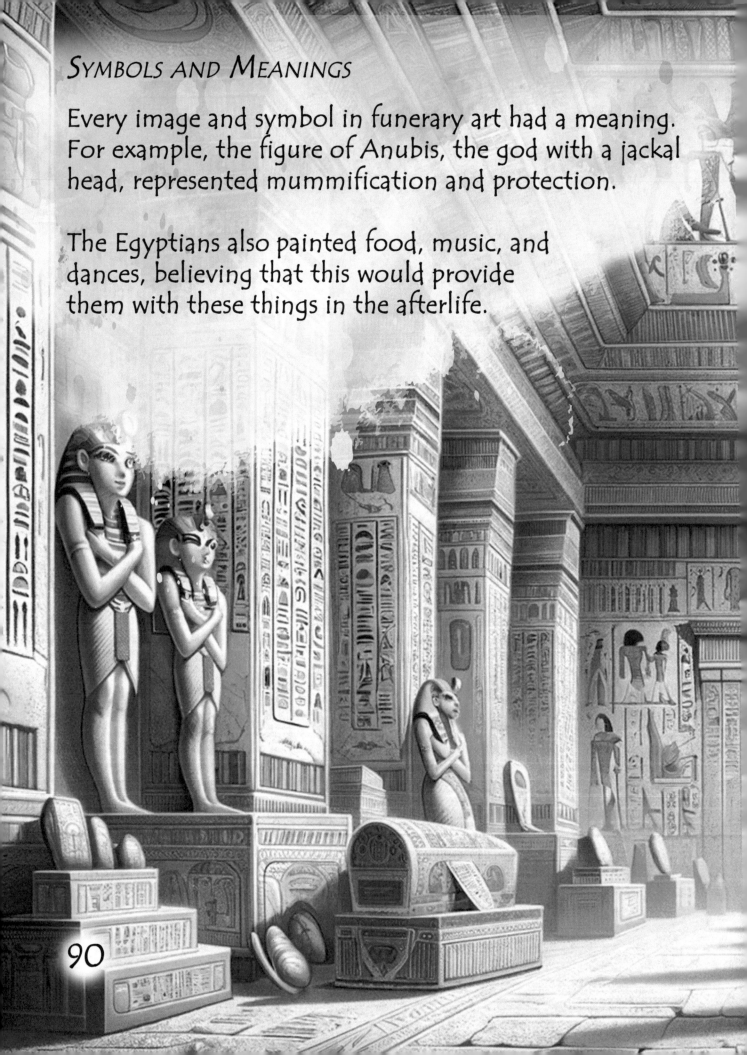

SYMBOLS AND MEANINGS

Every image and symbol in funerary art had a meaning. For example, the figure of Anubis, the god with a jackal head, represented mummification and protection.

The Egyptians also painted food, music, and dances, believing that this would provide them with these things in the afterlife.

90

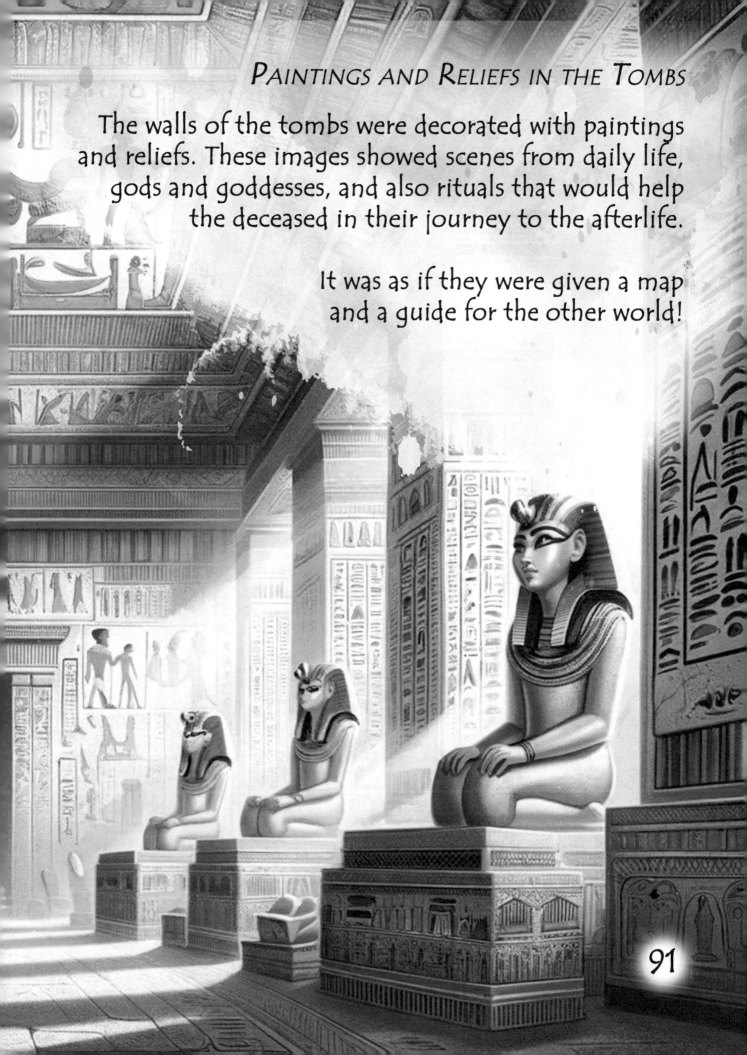

PAINTINGS AND RELIEFS IN THE TOMBS

The walls of the tombs were decorated with paintings and reliefs. These images showed scenes from daily life, gods and goddesses, and also rituals that would help the deceased in their journey to the afterlife.

It was as if they were given a map and a guide for the other world!

THE FAMOUS FUNERARY MASKS

The funerary masks, like the famous gold mask of Tutankhamun, are examples of the beautiful Egyptian funerary art.

These masks covered the face of the deceased and were believed to help protect their spirit and to recognize the body in the afterlife.

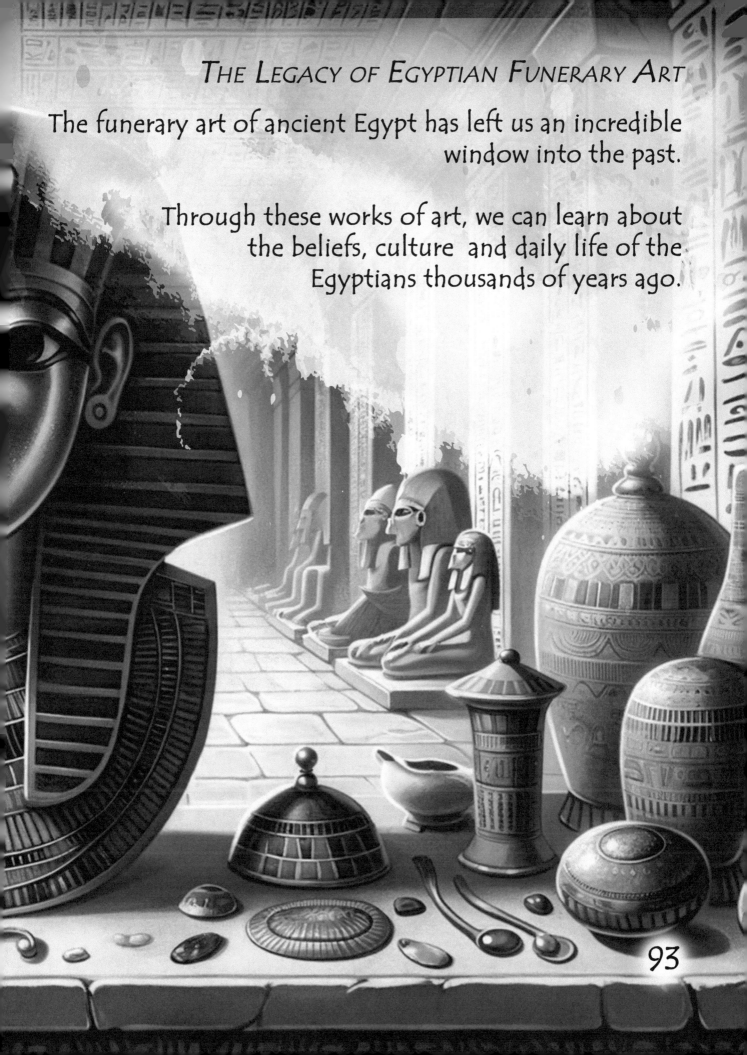

THE LEGACY OF EGYPTIAN FUNERARY ART

The funerary art of ancient Egypt has left us an incredible window into the past.

Through these works of art, we can learn about the beliefs, culture and daily life of the Egyptians thousands of years ago.

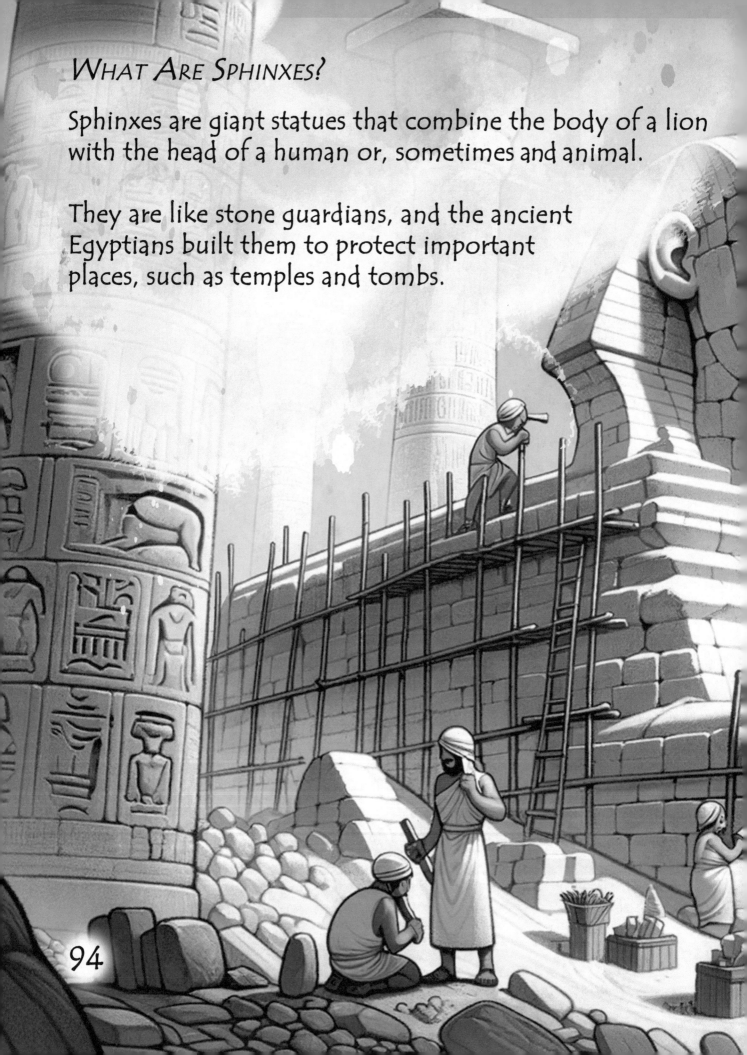

What Are Sphinxes?

Sphinxes are giant statues that combine the body of a lion with the head of a human or, sometimes and animal.

They are like stone guardians, and the ancient Egyptians built them to protect important places, such as temples and tombs.

94

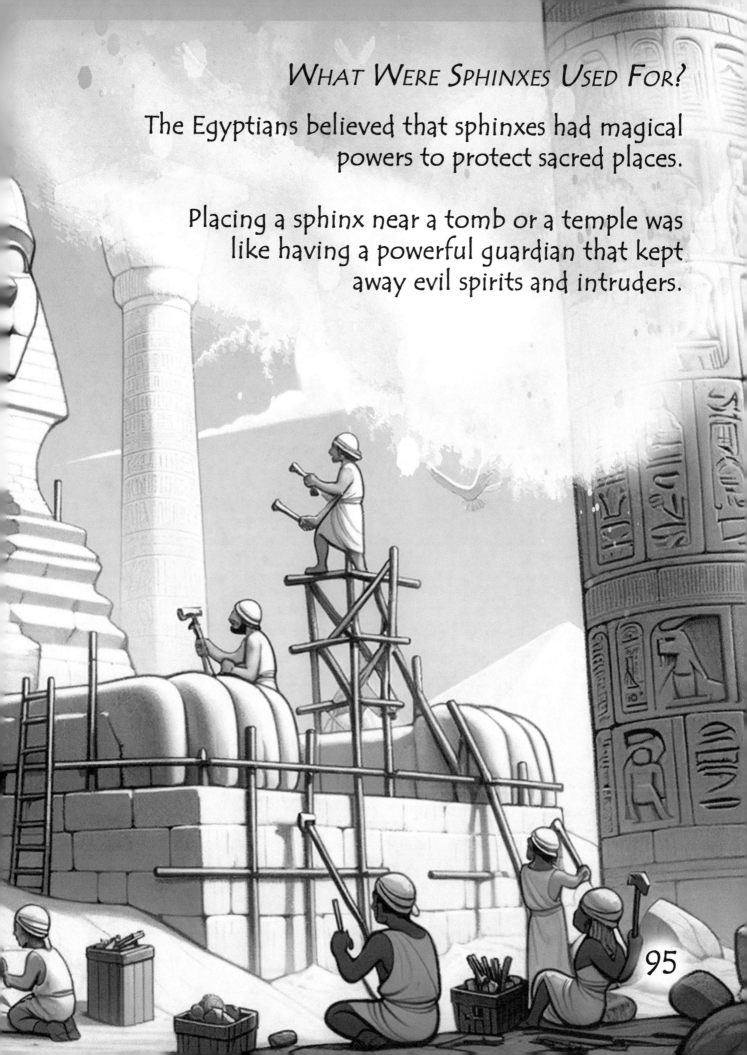

What Were Sphinxes Used For?

The Egyptians believed that sphinxes had magical powers to protect sacred places.

Placing a sphinx near a tomb or a temple was like having a powerful guardian that kept away evil spirits and intruders.

THE GREAT SPHINX OF GIZA

The most famous of all is the Great Sphinx of Giza. It's huge! It stands about 20 meters high, equivalent to a six-story building, and is about 73 meters long.

That's longer than a basketball court!

The Great Sphinx has the face of a man, believed to represent Pharaoh Khafre, and the body of a lion.

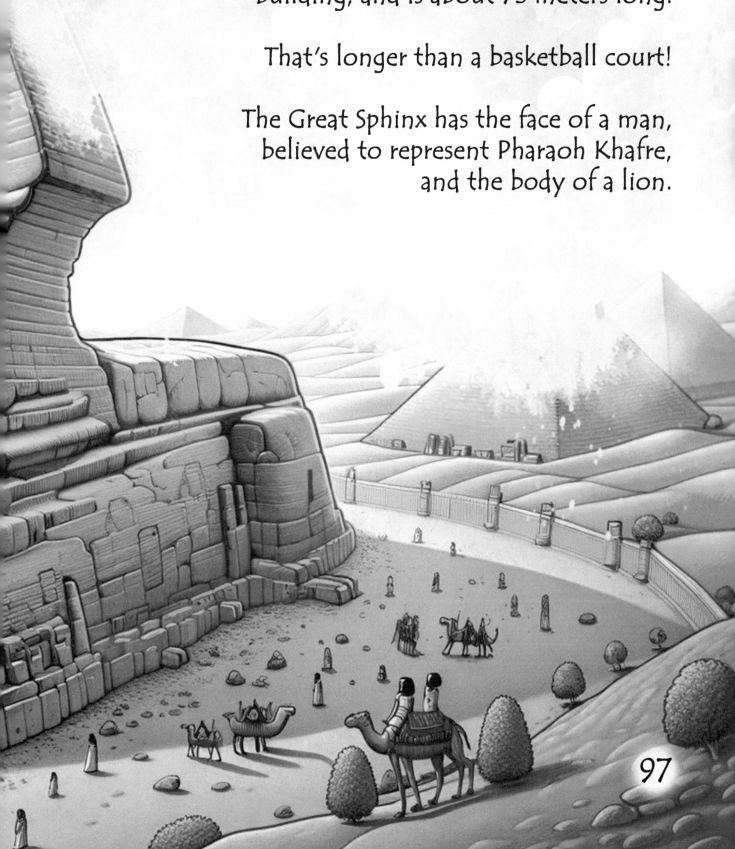

OTHER FAMOUS SPHINXES

Aside from the Great Sphinx of Giza, there are many other sphinxes in Egypt. Some are smaller and have the faces of pharaohs or gods.

They can be found in many places, such as at the entrances of temples or on the avenues leading to sacred sites.

THE LEGACY OF THE SPHINXES

Today, the sphinxes continue to be a powerful symbol of ancient Egypt.

They remind us of the greatness and mystery of a civilization that has fascinated the world for thousands of years.

WHAT ARE HIEROGLYPHS?

Hieroglyphs are a special type of writing used by the ancient Egyptians. They are not like the letters we use today. They are drawings and symbols that represent words or sounds.

Imagine writing a letter using drawings of animals, plants, and strange figures!

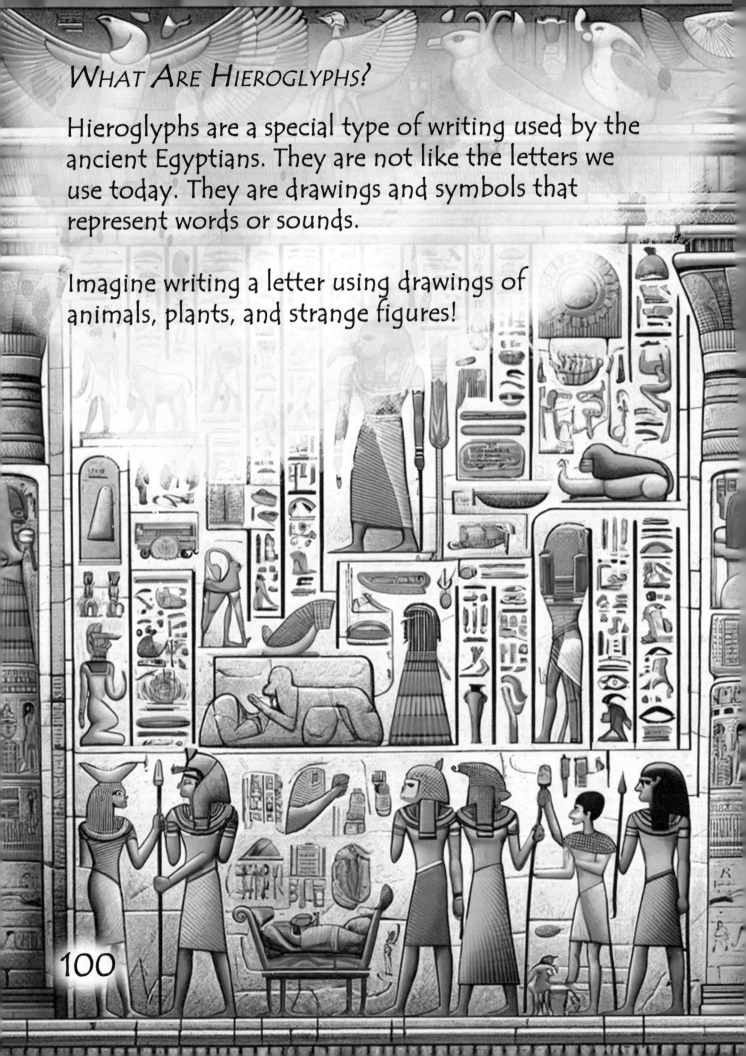

WHERE WERE HIEROGLYPHS USED?

The Egyptians wrote hieroglyphs in many places. They could be on the walls of temples, on the sides of sarcophagi, on papyri and even on small statues.

They used them to tell stories, record important events, and of course, for decoration.

101

THE ROSETTA STONE: THE KEY TO DECIPHERING

Everything changed with the discovery of the Rosetta Stone. This stone had the same text written in three different scripts: hieroglyphs, Demotic (another Egyptian script) and Greek.
Since experts could already read Greek, they were able to use it to understand hieroglyphs.

It was like finding the key to a secret treasure!

THE MYSTERY OF READING HIEROGLYPHS

For many years, after the Egyptian civilization disappeared, no one knew how to read hieroglyphs.

They became a great mystery. It was as if they had forgotten how to read a book full of wonderful stories.

A LANGUAGE OF IMAGES

Each hieroglyph was a small drawing with a meaning. They could represent simple things like the sun or water, but also more complicated ideas.

Some hieroglyphs were phonetic, meaning they represented sounds, like the letters in our alphabet.

104

THE LEGACY OF HIEROGLYPHS

Today, thanks to the Rosetta Stone and many years of study, we can understand the messages that the ancient Egyptians left behind.

Hieroglyphs open a window into their world, telling us about their gods, their beliefs, their daily life and their great pharaohs.

GAMES

Find the 7 Differences Between the Two Images:

Fill in the Following Crossword With the 6 Missing Words:

1. Object with which they covered the face of the deceased to protect the spirit.

2. Giant statue with the body of a lion and the head of a human.

3. Structure that served as a tomb for pharaohs and their families.

4. Type of writing that used drawings and symbols to represent words.

5. What objects were the tombs filled with the idea of using them after death.

6. Which god represents mummification and the protection of souls.

CREDITOS

Made in United States
Troutdale, OR
12/08/2024

26097222R00062